Endorsements

From the End Time to Heaven is a captivating, unique, logical and well-researched Neo-Evangelical examination of "the last days" based on Reverend Trapp's lifelong spiritual journey and work.

Reverend Trapp based this compelling read on four fundamental "pillars of truth": True Bible, True History, True Science, and True Common Sense, all of which traditional evangelicals have forgotten or ignored in the twenty-first century. Reverend Trapp clearly foretells the re-establishment of Israel and the emergence of the Antichrist, and outlines the eight signs of the End Time and the return of Christ through thorough research.

By providing numerous charts and maps, in keeping with Reverend Trapp's highly logical approach to his thesis, the reader is once again drawn and inspired by this work. It is obvious that Reverend Trapp was truly inspired by the Holy Spirit. Reverend Trapp is not so much warning us of the End Time but *informing and educating* us of the same.

I strongly recommend this book to everyone.

—William R. Richards, B.A., B.Ed.
Steinbach, Manitoba

Our journey as colleagues and friends started back in the early eighties in the community of Steinbach, Manitoba. I have had the blessing and privilege to know Rev. Werner Trapp, his wife Helen, and their children. Pastor Werner has been and still is faithful to the truth of the Word of God. With all his heart he believes that the Word is a lamp unto our feet and a light unto our path (Psalm 119:105). This revelation and understanding concerning the Word of life makes clear to all people the need of redemption in Christ Jesus.

Pastor Trapp has been raised up deeply anchored to his German heritage and language, which has seasoned him into writing this book. Plus, he has a deep walk in the fullness and filling power of the Holy Spirit. I believe this foundation of study and reflection has birthed forth this book *From the End Time to Heaven*. I believe his purpose is to help deepen and broaden people's hearts concerning Christ Jesus and the End Time, which many feel is near.

I also like the fifteen points that all believers should use as a foundation stone for Biblical research as one strives for deeper truth in God. I believe this book will be a good tool for people and students. It can lay out a path for them to go deeper in research about what they believe and hold to, concerning the Word of God historically and in teaching about the End Time.

As one reads this book, they will see that there is a collection of material that comes from a lifetime of travel and study. It shows a deep desire to know the full truth of Christ Jesus as Saviour and Lord, both historically and for the relevance of one's personal walk with Christ today here on earth. I believe it is a good starting point which gives one the research material to continue to build upon.

May you also enjoy and be challenged as you read *From the End Time to Heaven*. May it cause you to reflect and to walk deeper in your faith as you journey out your life as a believer here on earth with Christ Jesus.

—Rev. Dr. James Paul Humphries
Founder and Director of Project L.A.M.B.S. International

It is evident [Werner Trapp has] studied deeply on this topic of the End Time, beginning with Creation right through to the return of Jesus Christ to gather His loved ones to Himself for eternity.

I admit I do not fully understand the whole process and have not taken adequate time to research and study the timeline for His imminent return and all that is involved and surrounding it.

[Werner Trapp has] obviously scoured many sources for understanding and disclosure to arrive at [his] conclusions, relying on the Holy Spirit for guidance and understanding.

I have always acknowledged and upheld [Werner Trapp] as one who is fully committed to following [his] Lord and Saviour Jesus Christ, from many of our conversations over the years I have known [him].

This essay has certainly stimulated a desire to search deeper and seek to understand the End Time unfolding before our eyes.

—Jim Harms, B.A. Business, B.A. Ethics
YFC Steinbach and long-time friend of Brother Werner Trapp

For many decades [Werner Trapp] has worked intensively and precisely with the Bible, always gaining new insights and extensively documenting the knowledge [he] has gained with comparisons of texts from the Old Testament and New Testament and formulating it in [his] publications.

I am very impressed by [Werner Trapp's] competent interpretation of the Bible. I would call it [his] life's work.

—Erika Roeske-Schwiede
Primary School Teacher/Vice-Principal
Wiesbaden, Germany

While I do not agree with everything in it, I am impressed by the amount of research that Werner Trapp did for his latest book. His lifetime of faithful ministry service means that we should take his work seriously.

—Michael Zwaagstra, M.Ed., M.A.
High School Teacher, City Councillor, Newspaper Columnist
Author of *A Sage on the Stage: Common Sense Reflections on Teaching and Learning*
(John Catt Educational, 2020)

From the End Time to Heaven

A Neo-Evangelical Viewpoint

Rev. Werner Trapp, BBR

FROM THE END TIME TO HEAVEN
Copyright © 2023 by Rev. Werner Trapp, BBR

All rights reserved. Neither this publication nor any part of this publication may be reproduced or transmitted in any form or by any means, electronic or mechanical, including photocopying, recording or any information storage and retrieval system, without permission in writing from the author.

Unless otherwise indicated, all scripture taken from the New King James Version®. Copyright © 1982 by Thomas Nelson, Inc. Used by permission. All rights reserved.

ISBN: 978-1-4866-2303-7
eBook ISBN: 978-1-4866-2304-4

Word Alive Press
119 De Baets Street Winnipeg, MB R2J 3R9
www.wordalivepress.ca

Cataloguing in Publication information can be obtained from Library and Archives Canada.

Contents

LIST OF FIGURES	vii
PREFACE	xi
WORD OF THANKS	xiii
NEO-EVANGELICALS AND THEIR VIEWS	xv
MY METHODS OF BIBLICAL INTERPRETATION	xvii
THE STORY ABOUT FINDING ESCHATOLOGICAL IMAGES ON THE MAP OF EUROPE	xxi

FROM THE END TIME TO HEAVEN:
INTRODUCTION — 1

THE FIRST SIGN OF THE END TIME AND RETURN OF JESUS CHRIST:
THE RE-ESTABLISHMENT OF ISRAEL — 5

THE SECOND SIGN OF THE END TIME AND RETURN OF JESUS CHRIST:
THE COMING OF THE ANTI-CHRISTIAN EMPIRE — 13

THE THIRD SIGN OF THE END TIME AND RETURN OF JESUS CHRIST:
FINDING THE REAL ANTICHRIST — 21

THE FOURTH SIGN OF THE END TIME AND RETURN OF JESUS CHRIST:
FINDING THE FALSE PROPHET — 33

THE FIFTH SIGN OF THE END TIME AND RETURN OF JESUS CHRIST:
THE GREAT FALLING AWAY — 45

THE SIXTH SIGN OF THE END TIME AND RETURN OF JESUS CHRIST:
THE QUICK SPREAD OF BIBLICAL CHRISTIANITY IN THE WORLD — 47

THE SEVENTH SIGN OF THE END TIME AND RETURN OF JESUS CHRIST:
THE GREAT TRIBULATION — 49

THE EIGHTH SIGN OF THE END TIME AND RETURN OF JESUS CHRIST: **THE RETURN OF JESUS CHRIST**	**55**
END TIME TO HEAVEN: **WHAT HAPPENS IMMEDIATELY AFTER CHRIST'S RETURN**	**61**
END TIME TO HEAVEN II: **THE MILLENNIUM**	**63**
END TIME TO HEAVEN III: **THE GREAT WHITE THRONE JUDGMENT**	**67**
END TIME TO HEAVEN IV: **FINALLY IN HEAVEN!**	**71**
APPENDIX: **Other Important Topics**	**75**
THE CORRECT DATES OF JESUS CHRIST'S LIFE AND PENTECOST (Written in 2017)	77
SEVENTY LIES, MISCONCEPTIONS, AND HERESIES CIRCULATED AMONG EVANGELICALS	83
FALLACIES OF THE PRE-TRIBULATION RAPTURE THEORY	95
MISTRANSLATED BIBLE VERSES	99
ONE OF THE GREATEST SPIRITUAL EVENTS OF THE TWENTIETH CENTURY	103
REFERENCES	107
BIBLIOGRAPHY	109
ABOUT THE AUTHOR	111

LIST OF FIGURES

1: Globe	ix
2: Eschatological Images Superimposed on the Map of Europe	xxiii
3: The Extent of Antichrist's Domain	9
4: 1935–2021 Significant Earthquakes 5.0+	11
5: The Great Image of Nebuchadnezzar	17
6: Italy—The Centre of Antichrist's Empire	19
7: San Marino—The Antichrist Before His Assassination	25
8: Jutland—The Antichrist After His Assassination	27
9: Greece—Six Toes and Crippled Arm	29
10: The Coat of Arms of San Marino	31
11: England—The Head of the "Great Harlot"	37
12: Netherlands—The Hand of the "Great Harlot"	39
13: The Golden Cup	41
14: The Black Sea—The "Dragon's Head"	43
15: Chronological Chart of Events in Revelation	53
16: Scandinavia—The Lion of Judah	59
17: Possible Model of Caravansary	81

Figure 1. The End Time struggle between Jesus Christ and Antichrist is represented in picture form on the map of Europe. God accomplished this during the formation of the continents.

NOTES

PREFACE

DEAR READER, YOU are about to read a presentation of the End Time story that runs differently to any other book on the same theme you have ever read. The reason is that this book attempts to look upon the End Time through the eyes, understanding, and worldview of the ancient biblical writers as much as possible. It actually should be understood so by us too, in contrast to our modern understanding and worldview of today, which view I consider to be wrong. *This book also contains eleven new propositions about the End Time, some of which were only recently discovered.*

In this book, the Holy Spirit gave me eleven new discoveries.

1. There are eleven eschatological images on the map of Europe.

2. The true name of the Antichrist.

3. The miniature state of San Marino will be the Antichrist's entry into world politics.

4. The coat of arms of San Marino contains the number 666 inverted.

5. A ruler and his territory are seen as one unit in the eschatological texts of the Bible.

6. Great Tribulation Christians can know the exact return date of the Lord Jesus Christ.

7. Why lost spirits will suffer eternally.

8. Heaven is a planet.

9. The New Jerusalem will not look like a cube, but like a pyramid.

10. The amazing grace of God at the Great White Throne Judgment.

11. That the empires of Revelation chapters twelve, thirteen, and sixteen are one and the same as in Daniel two and seven.

NOTES

WORD OF THANKS

I APPRECIATE MY dear wife for her patience during the time it took to write this book. I thank my son Eberhardt for the work he has done to produce a draft copy of this book, for creating the images, and for giving me useful ideas to incorporate into it. I also thank my editor at Word Alive Press, Matthew Knight, Ph.D., for his thoughtful review and superb work. Foremost, I thank the Holy Spirit for guiding me through this study. He helped me to discover a lot of things which I did not know through my own knowledge. I could not have written this book without His help.

Rev. Werner Trapp, BBR

NEO-EVANGELICALS AND THEIR VIEWS

THE VIEWS OF Neo-Evangelicals ("New Evangelicals") began with Harold Ockenga, Carl F. H. Henry, and Dr. Billy Graham.

Harold Ockenga was a leading figure of mid-twentieth century American Evangelicalism. He was a part of the reform movement known as "Neo-Evangelicalism." Ockenga was a Congregational minister who served for many years as a lead pastor of Park Street Church in Boston, Massachusetts.

Carl F. H. Henry was Dean of Fuller Theological Seminary. He was an American Evangelical theologian who provided intellectual and institutional leadership to the Neo-Evangelical movement from the mid-twentieth century onward.

Billy Graham was a world-renowned Neo-Evangelical evangelist of the twentieth century who led millions around the world to accept Christ as their personal Saviour and Lord.

Ockenga explained that the Neo-Evangelical movement was intended to face intellectual problems and meet them in the framework of modern learning. At present many Evangelical theological schools accept and teach Neo-Evangelical concepts. Neo-Evangelicals also started the monthly magazine "Christianity Today," which has become a widely read and accepted publication.

Neo-Evangelicals experience a persecution and defamation by their Evangelical opponents similar to that experienced by the Pentecostals at the beginning of the twentieth century, though Neo-Evangelicals strive to be theologically correct and in line with the Bible.

In contrast to traditional Evangelicals, Neo-Evangelicals accept honest and true scientific statements in regards to creation and Biblical exegesis, which are rejected by a lot of traditional Evangelicals.

Traditional Evangelicals try to unify the creation stories of Genesis chapters one and two, an approach which Neo-Evangelicals consider naïve, incorrect, and not really possible. The traditional Evangelical position about creation turns intellectual people off from believing in God and the Bible as the inspired word of God. Neo-Evangelicals accept that these two creation stories represent two separate creations, a point which agrees with true science. The creation of mankind in Genesis chapter one is a far older and a different creation than the one described in Genesis chapter two. The original creation of today's people (Homo Sapiens) happened two or three hundred thousand years ago in the Horn of Africa, according to natural science. This is what Genesis chapter one is all about. According to natural science, white Europeans appeared about 4,500 years ago, in accord with the Bible, which describes them in Genesis 5:32 as descendants of Noah's son Japheth. That Japheth is the father of the Europeans is demonstrated in Genesis 10:2–5: *"The sons of Japheth were Gomer, Magog [Russians], Madai [Medes], Javan [Greeks], Tubal Mesech [Russians], and Thiras."* His son Gomer was the father of Ashkenas, the Jewish name for Germans. The text further mentions that some of these tribes were living on the islands and coastal areas of the Mediterranean Sea—namely, Europe. These tribal names prove that Japheth was the father of the Europeans.

In Genesis chapter one, God created male and female mankind simultaneously by His word (verse 27), as He had done with all other things in that chapter. In Genesis chapter two, the earth already exists. In this chapter, we see that God created Adam about six thousand years ago in a very different way. He molded the form of Adam's body out of the red dry dust of the Middle Eastern steppe with His own hands and wetted the dust—probably with His tears, in reference to Adam's future fall into sin, so we are the product of red dust and the tears of God's eyes. He awoke Adam (the Red One) to life with a kiss according to Genesis chapter two as indicated in verse 7, which says, *"and [God] breathed into his nostrils the breath of life…"* One cannot breathe air into another person's nose without touching his lips. This was the kiss of son-ship, which is why Adam is called *"the son of God"* in Luke 3:38.

In Genesis chapter two, God invites Adam, like any father would do with his son, to take part in His work, here by letting Adam name the animals God created (verses 19–20). God's intent was to show Adam His creational powers by letting him see God at His creational work.

Then God created the woman by removing a rib from Adam's body (Genesis 2:21–22), and built her, apparently in the same way as Adam's body, with His hands. There is some humour in this story of the woman's creation. According to the Jewish history writer Josephus (about 75 A.D.), reflecting Jewish beliefs, Adam had seen the lovemaking and sexual acts of the animals which happened some time after their creation, and he wanted to experience the same. That is why God complied with Adam's wishes and created Eve.

Neo-Evangelicals maintain that Evangelicals treat the historical and eschatological texts of the Bible incorrectly by looking at them from our modern understanding, while they should be looked at from the writers' understanding (the fourteenth rule of Evangelical Bible interpretation states that historical and eschatological texts should be viewed from the writers' understanding, not ours—for more on these rules, keep reading). For example, the book of Revelation should be looked at from the perspective of its writer John and not ours. This approach will lead us to different insights than what traditional Evangelicals now endorse. My presentation "From the End Time to Heaven" is based on Neo-Evangelical principles, and you will learn things which are theologically correct according to the Bible, though they may be new to you.

MY METHODS OF BIBLICAL INTERPRETATION

I FOLLOW EXACTLY the Evangelical rules of Scripture interpretation that I recite here:

    A. The biblical text must be interpreted honestly in the light of context, language, biblical history, biblical tradition, general teaching, typological meaning, and dispensational location.

    B. Twelve Rules for Bible Exegesis (Dake, *Dake's Annotated Reference Bible*, 1963)

        1. Be fluent in the language of your Bible. Know the grammar of your language and use it also in regard to the Bible.

        2. Give the word of the Bible the same meaning as in other books.

        3. Be fluent in biblical customs and traditions.

        4. Be familiar with the geography of biblical lands.

        5. Be familiar with the important kingdoms and people mentioned in the Bible.

        6. Be familiar with the general redemption plan of God.

        7. Be familiar with the three classes of humanity in the Bible: the Israelites, the Gentiles, and Christians.

        8. Be familiar with the historical background of every book of the Bible.

        9. Never exchange a literal meaning of a Scripture portion with a symbolic or a spiritual meaning. Take everything literally unless the text wants to be understood differently. Even symbolic texts have a literal background.

10. Use a good concordance for your Bible research.

11. Be just as intelligent with the Bible text as you would be with any other book.

12. Generally, the Bible does not contradict itself.

I myself have added the following rules to these twelve:

13. Compare text with text of the same context. The Bible explains itself.

14. Understand the historical and prophetical statements of the Bible the way the writers of the Bible have understood them. Do not interpret them according to our modern view.

15. Search historical and prophetic texts through the eyes of a Scotland Yard Detective looking for incidental evidence.

Sadly, many Evangelical pastors do not always follow these rules. Here are a few examples:

Creation

Most Evangelicals believe that the Bible states that the earth was created six thousand years ago. This is not true. There is not one Bible verse that maintains such. The belief that the earth was created six thousand years ago stems from the English bishop James Ussher (1581–1656). He counted the generations from Jesus Christ back to Adam as given in the Bible and arrived at 4,004 B.C. for the creation of Adam. This is how the conflict arose between Bible believers and true science. True science does tell us that the earth is a lot older than six thousand years, and the Bible itself does not contradict this. The creation recounted in Genesis chapter one happened a lot earlier than six thousand years ago. This account ends with the creation of the human race. The first ethnic group was the Africans, followed by the Asians. However, the European and Semitic races came up after Noah, some 4,344 years ago. The creation in Genesis chapter two is a different creation, which took place on the dry land of the Middle East where God made Adam from the red dust of the area and showed him His creative powers by creating animals in front of him. Adam's ethnicity cannot be determined.

Adam is called the *"Son of God"* according to Luke 3:38. Looking at the entire story of Genesis chapter two, one gets the impression that Adam was created to bring redemption to the older human races, for the care of the Tree of Life was given to him in trust (Genesis 2:15). He would not need the many fruits of the whole tree for himself, so the fruit of this tree was meant to be shared with more people. In the fall into sin, Adam lost his redemptive calling and needed redemption himself. That is where God's redemptive plan through our Lord Jesus Christ came into effect.

The True Meaning of the Word "Earth"

According to the fourteenth rule of Evangelical Bible interpretation, the word "earth" in the Bible must be understood the way the writers of the Bible understood it. To them, the "earth" had Jerusalem at its centre, and to the west it reached to the Atlantic Ocean past Spain and up to Britain, to the north it extended through Europe to Germany, and to the east up to India, although they also knew about the "Silk Road" leading to China. In the south it reached into Africa up to Ethiopia.

The Words "All," "the Whole," "Entire," and Like Words

These words in the Bible must be understood the way the writers of the Holy Scriptures understood them. For instance, Daniel 2:39 reads: *"…after you shall arise another kingdom inferior to yours; then another, a third kingdom of bronze, which shall rule over all the earth."* Today we know that this is not true, but Daniel and his audience did not know better. This is a problem you often find in the Bible. For instance, see the book of Revelation chapter thirteen, where it is said that the *"authority was given him over every tribe, tongue, and nation"* (v. 7). When considering the information available to the Biblical writers, you get a different perspective, and you will see the truth of the matter that Antichrist does not rule over all the nations of the earth as we know it today.

If someone interprets Revelation 13 based on the knowledge we have of the world today, that person creates a contradiction with Daniel 2, where it clearly states that the last empire, which will be destroyed by the Kingdom of God, encompasses only ten nations. The modern interpretation that claims the whole world as we know it today will be part of Antichrist's kingdom is therefore clearly seen to be false. Any interpretation of what the Lord Jesus says about the end time in Matthew 24, Mark 13, Luke 17, and Luke 21 cannot go beyond the scope of Daniel 2.

Any statement in the Bible must be viewed within the limits of Daniel's prophecy in Daniel 2. Some additional scripture references are 1 Thessalonians 4:13-17, 2 Thessalonians 2:, Revelation 13: and more.

Finally, my Bible exposition is built up on these four pillars of truth: 1. True Bible, 2. True History, 3. True Science, and 4. True Common Sense.

THE STORY ABOUT FINDING ESCHATOLOGICAL IMAGES ON THE MAP OF EUROPE

IN 1968 I was looking upon the map of Europe when the Holy Ghost drew my attention to some of its features that resemble images. Right away I saw that these images resemble things referring to the second coming of the Lord Jesus Christ. I wondered why nobody else had ever found this out. It appears that we all look at that map with some sort of blindness, because these images are so easy to recognize.

I will start to look at them from the north.

First, examine the Scandinavian Peninsula. It looks similar to a lion. Indeed, the Swedes know this and call it "the Lion of the North." It is image number three on the map. This fits exactly to Revelation 5:5, *"…the Lion of the tribe of Judah…"* as well as Job 37:22, which says of God, *"He comes from the north…"* Then tightly snuggled to it is the Baltic Sea, which looks like a platypus, the Australian mammal that has a duck's bill for a mouth, so it appears like a double-natured creature. The Holy Ghost told me that this platypus picture represents the two natures of our Lord Jesus: both God and man.

Then the Holy Ghost led me to look at the Danish peninsula of Jutland. It looks like a small man's face with a horn on top. I was told that this image represents Antichrist (Daniel 7:8). The Danes in fact call it "the little man." On the map of Europe, it looks like the Lion of Judah attacks Antichrist (see image number four on the map).

Then the Holy Ghost pointed out the features of England (without Scotland). It looks like a woman's face, where the estuary of the river Thames resembles her mouth, and I was told that she represents the Great Harlot Babylon of Revelation 18–19. This image is number five on the map.

The next image on the map of Europe is the Netherlands, which looks like the hand of the Harlot Babylon pointing toward Antichrist (Jutland). This is image number six on the map.

Then follows the border of France with Germany and Switzerland. The Holy Ghost pointed out that this stretch of border looks like half of a chalice. If one imagines the other half on France's territory, one can see the full cup. It represents Babylon's cup of Revelation 18:6 (image number seven on the map).

A very clear image is Italy. It resembles a military boot. The Holy Ghost pointed out that on the map it looks like the island Sicily is acting like the stone of Daniel 2:45 hitting the foot of Italy, which represents the ten nations the stone is breaking into pieces. On the map this picture is images one and two.

Greece on the map of Europe has two images. The first one is the peninsula Achaia that faces the sea with the likeness of a dragon's forearm with six toes. The Holy Ghost led me to 2 Samuel 21:20, describing a man of great stature who had six fingers on each hand. This feature was characteristic of the giants in King David's time. This image is number nine on the map.

It is closely related to the image on the Greek peninsula Chalcidice of three fingers on a crippled arm, which is image number ten on the map, corresponding to Zechariah 11:17, which describes what will happen to the "worthless shepherd" (Antichrist): *"A sword shall be against his arm and against his right eye; his arm shall completely wither, and his right eye shall be totally blinded."*

The Black Sea looks like a dragon's head with horns without an eye on its right side. It actually represents two images in one. First, the dragon's head represents the False Prophet, the religious partner of Antichrist, who spoke like a dragon (Revelation 13:11). Second, the blind eye in the Black Sea references Antichrist (see the previous paragraph). This combination points to the intimate relationship between Antichrist and the False Prophet. One more point is that this image represents Revelation 13:12: *"And he [the False Prophet] exercises all the authority of the first beast in his presence..."* This is image number eight on the map. The dragon faces east and makes the whole anti-Christian image walk toward Russia and Israel.

Finally, there is another image representing Antichrist in the border of the microstate San Marino in Italy, which looks like a man's face looking east with a small horn on his head. It is too small to appear on the map of Europe, but appears later in this book.

Why are there two images for Antichrist on the map of Europe? My take is that the image of Jutland represents Antichrist as a powerful politician and shows Christ attacking him, while the face on San Marino's border represents Antichrist as a small political power before his assassination. On the map of Europe the "Lion of the North" is far bigger than all other images, indicating that He will be the victor.

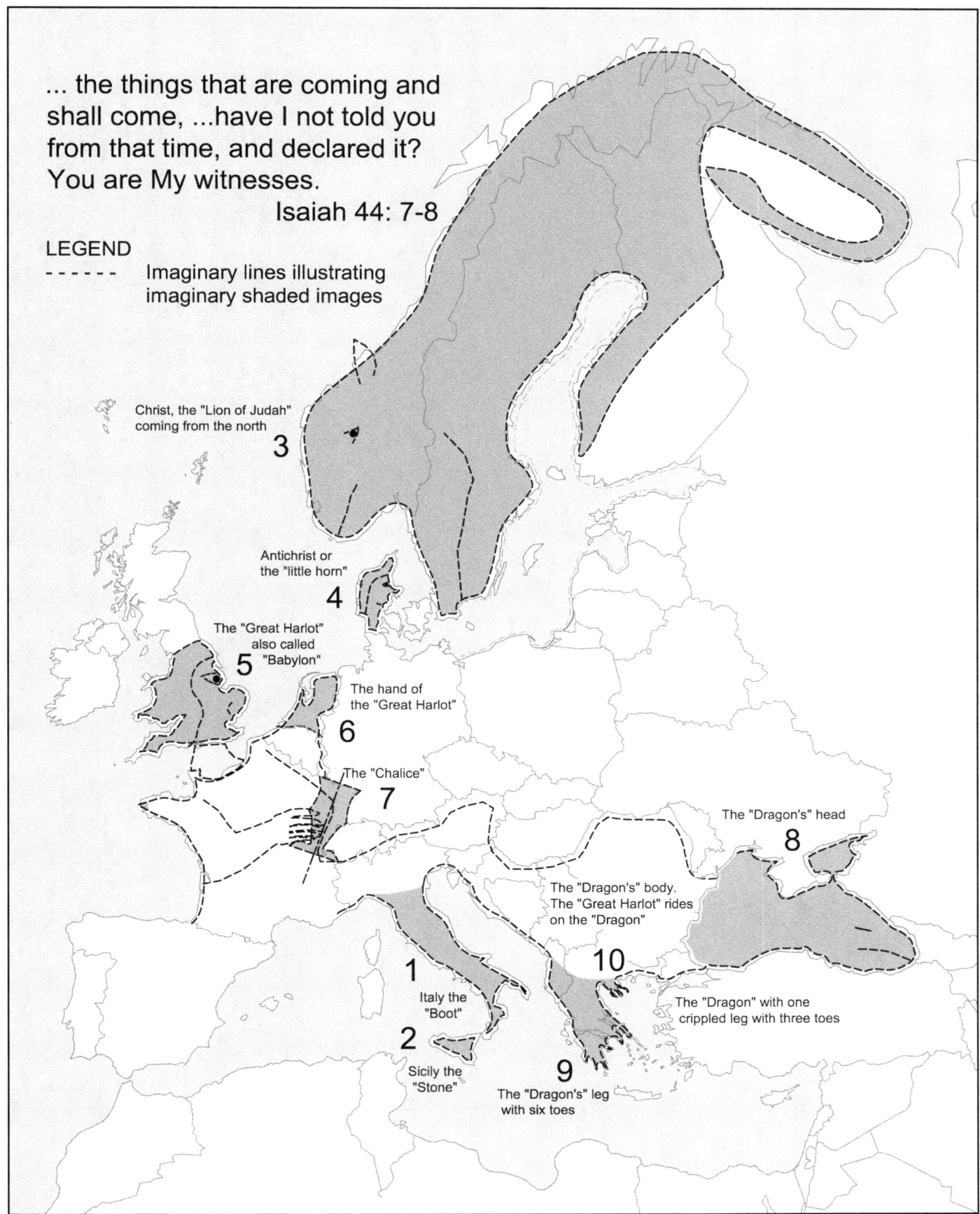

Figure 2: Eschatological Images Superimposed on the Map of Europe

NOTES

FROM THE END TIME TO HEAVEN:
INTRODUCTION

My Qualification for this Study

I HAVE FOUR and a half years of theological training at the following schools: Eichenkreuzhaus Seminary of the Evangelical Young Men's Society (Kassel, Germany), the Northwest Bible College (Edmonton, AB), the Moody Bible Institute (Chicago, IL), Steinbach Bible College (Steinbach, MB), Billy Graham School of Evangelism (Wheaton College, IL), and Bible Research International (Cambridge, ON), where I earned my Bachelor of Bible Research (BBR) degree.

I have experienced four divine revelations of God which guarantee that there is indeed a living God. I present one of these occasions here.

In the spring of 1955, I was awakened from my midnight sleep by a loud voice calling me by my name: *"Werner!"* I assumed that my wife was talking to me, but she denied it. I was called a second time, and again my wife denied having called me by my name. Then I remembered how the prophet Samuel was called in 1 Samuel 3:4–10, and I waited for the third call. Indeed it came, and I answered like Samuel: *"Speak, Lord, your servant hears."* God told me to go to Communist East Germany to preach the Gospel there.

I was terrified and told God, "Please send me wherever you wish, but please do not send me to East Germany, because I will not remain a free man there for three days. They will arrest me and put me into a concentration camp very quickly." I fought against God until the morning sun rose, but God did not give in. Finally I surrendered and told God, "Okay, I will go, but I will leave my family here in Canada, and you will have to open the door for this mission." He never did open that door, so I assume that He wanted to test my commitment to Him. Of course, there was no chance of someone hiding in our bedroom to fool me in this matter, and neither was there an electronic device that could have fooled me, so the fact remains that the living God spoke to me indeed. God still sent me east from Medicine Hat, Alberta to serve East European German people in Steinbach, Manitoba. Thus God leads!

Because this study contains many Bible references, we need to first establish the truthfulness of the Bible's inspiration. During the last 190 years, the Bible was critically researched by scholars of "Higher Criticism" who themselves had no personal encounter with the living Christ, and therefore the Bible was a closed book to them. They are to be blamed for many people losing faith in the Bible. Sadly, most of these theological scholars were Germans. The consequence was that the person of the Lord Jesus Christ, His deity, and His mission were attacked. The Lord Jesus was no longer conceived by the Holy Ghost, but by a Roman soldier who raped Mary.

He never died for our sins and never rose from the dead, nor did He ascend into heaven. These things were all fables invented by His disciples.

True Evangelical churches still cling to the traditional creeds beginning with the Apostolic Creed to the Confirmation of our Faith of Chicago, IL (1978), where the full inspiration of the Bible was confirmed.

Who Has the Facts?

Evangelical scholars found about twenty thousand spelling mistakes within the more than six thousand ancient Bible copies, and also about 170 contradictions. Many of these contradictions are retained in most translations. Some of these contradictions can be solved, as for example the one in Galatians 6:2 & 5: *"Bear one another's burdens, and so fulfill the law of Christ"* against *"For each one shall bear his own load."* Paul gives the general position of the law of Christ in verse 2, and in verse 5 he addresses the problem of one that might burden the congregation unnecessarily instead of carrying his own share of the load. Or take for example Acts 2:17–18, where women are to prophesy (preach) even as men do, against 1 Corinthians 14:34–35 and 1 Timothy 2:12, which deal with the problem of women interrupting the service by calling on their husbands to explain things to them. This is what Paul criticizes. These are two different issues, both occurring at the same time as proved by Acts 21:8–9, where the evangelist Philip has four daughters who prophesy. So it could be possible that other contradictions also can be solved. The reason why copyists retained these contradictions is that they considered them to be a part of divine inspiration. It is actually surprising that more contradictions do not appear in the biblical text. After all, the writers of the Bible were imperfect persons like everybody else.

None of these mistakes and contradictions have any influence on biblical doctrines. These contradictions amount to 0.3% of the whole biblical text—less than 1%, only three in one thousand Bible verses!

God has used well-educated men like the prophet Isaiah as well as primitive shepherds like the prophet Amos to present His message to us. Therefore, we find far fewer spelling mistakes in the book of Isaiah than in the book of Amos. We are indebted to the conscientious work of the ancient copyists that more contradictions are not found in the biblical text. It is said that a newly finished copy of a scripture scroll was tested by counting the number of letters that appeared in it. If the resulting test showed a mismatch in the number of letters compared to the original, the entire new scroll was rejected and burned. Among these ancient copyists we find the men of Qumran (150 BC–100 AD) and the Masoretes (600–800 AD). The Apostle Paul says it right in 2 Corinthians 4:7 when he writes, *"...we have this treasure in earthen vessels, that the excellence of the power may be of God and not of us."* The earthen vessels are the copyists, and the power of God is the divine inspiration of the text.

For example, compare your modern Bible translation with the original text of the Qumran scroll of 150 BC translated into English as Daniel 2:36–45. Daniel reveals and explains a dream that the Babylonian king Nebuchadnezzar had dreamed but forgotten.

> This was the dream; now we will tell its interpretation in the king's presence. You, O king, are the king of kings, to whom the God of heaven has given the kingdom, the power, the might, and the glory; into whose hand he has given, wherever they dwell, human beings, the wild animals, and the birds of the air, and whom he has made ruler over them all—you are the head of gold. After you shall arise another kingdom inferior to yours, and a third kingdom of bronze, which shall rule over the entire earth. Then there shall be a fourth kingdom, strong as iron; just as iron crushes and shatters everything, it shall crush and smash all these,

like iron which crushes, all the earth. Just as you saw the feet and toes partly of potter's clay and partly of iron, it shall be a divided kingdom; but some of the hardness of iron shall be in it, as you saw the iron mixed with common clay. Just as the toes of the feet were partly iron and partly clay, so the kingdom shall be partly strong and partly brittle. And just as you saw the iron mixed with clay, so they will intermingle with one another in marriage, but they will not hold together, just as iron does not mix with clay.

And in the days of those kings the God of heaven will set up a kingdom which shall never be destroyed, nor shall its sovereignty be delivered to another people. It shall crush all these kingdoms and put an end to them, and it shall stand forever; Just as you saw that a stone was hewn from the mountain by no human hand, and that it crushed the iron, the bronze, the clay, the silver, and the gold. A great God has revealed to the king what shall be in the future. The dream is certain, and its interpretation is reliable. (Abegg, Flint, & Ulrich, 1999, *The Dead Sea Scrolls Bible*)

The sentences may run differently in your modern Bible. However, the content is exactly the same as in the 2,150-year-old scroll found in a cave at Qumran at the Dead Sea in Israel.

This is just a small example that witnesses to the trustworthiness of the modern Bible. More than six thousand ancient copies exist that show the same facts. No question, this is a great miracle! The Spirit of God was at work here. However, due to the mistakes and contradictions found one cannot honestly say that every word in the Bible is "God-breathed inspiration" and that the Bible is without mistakes. I repeat—in spite of these mistakes, the Bible is still a trustworthy book that you can depend on.

On the basis of these findings, some German, Swedish, and Danish Bibles I have read have corrected the text of 2 Timothy 3:16 from reading *"All Scripture is given by inspiration of God"* to reading *"All scripture <u>that</u> is inspired by God."*

Adam Clarke, Bible scholar and commentator, puts it like this.

> "All Scripture is given by inspiration of God"—This sentence is not well translated; the original πασα γραφη θεοκνευστος ωφιλιμος προς διδασκαλιαν, κ. τ. λ. should be rendered: "Every writing *divinely inspired* is profitable for doctrine," etc. The particle και, and, *is omitted by almost all the versions and many of the fathers,* and certainly does not agree well with the text. (Clarke, n.d.)

THE FIRST SIGN OF THE END TIME AND RETURN OF JESUS CHRIST:
THE RE-ESTABLISHMENT OF ISRAEL

THERE ARE *THREE historical happenings* that show that the End Time is in progress right now:

   a. The first time when the ten nations of Daniel 2:41–44 appeared together in history after the end of the old Roman Empire. This happened in 1918 when Yugoslavia was first established. These nations are historically a part of Daniel's prophecy in verses 31–40: Spain, Britain (not Scotland), France, Italy, Austria, Greece, Bulgaria, Romania, Albania, and Yugoslavia. These ten countries were provinces in the former Roman Empire. These nations can be seen as the children of Rome, while the other countries on that same territory were created during the Middle Ages, like Portugal from Spain, for example. These newer countries can be seen as the grandchildren of Rome, and they do not belong to the ten nations of Daniel chapter 2:41–44. There are no others.

   b. The founding of the present State of Israel in 1948.

   c. The day that Israel occupied Old Jerusalem in 1967.

These three points combined are *the first sign that the End Time has arrived.*

The ten nations listed above will become the imminent new anti-Christian Roman Empire. Some people reckon that the European Union is that empire. It encompassed twenty-seven nations as of 2022, but it will break up, because a lot of people in Germany and other countries are unhappy with this union and wish to leave it, as Britain recently did. There will be a shift of association within the union and a new state union will rise that encompasses the ten nations, becoming the new anti-Christian Roman Empire according to Daniel 2:31–44.

In this chapter I will focus on points b and c above, which deal with the founding of the State of Israel in 1948.

Evangelicals have historically accepted the heretical teaching of the Roman Catholic Church that with the resurrection of Christ, God has cursed the Jewish people and transferred all promises of God pertaining to them to the Church, which is now the Israel of God.

This heresy is at the root of the incredible human sufferings that have been imposed upon Jewish people throughout Christian history, from the second century into the present. They were pushed from country to country, called "pigs" and "Christ murderers." They were blamed for pestilences created by poisoning water wells. Jews were accused of using the blood of Gentile babies for their Passover wine. They were forbidden to exercise a trade, and so were forced to concentrate on financial businesses for a livelihood. European princes forced the Jews to live in ghettos in their cities. Whenever they needed money, they would raid the ghettos and rob Jews of their money and valuables. This antisemitism found its crowning crime in the concentration death camps of the Nazis, who were bent on eradicating the Jewish race.

This treatment of Jewish people contradicts the Christian obligation to "love your neighbour." Therefore, it was a great shame for the Christian Church to have promoted antisemitism.

In contrast, the Apostle Paul writes in Romans 9:4, *"[They are] Israelites, to whom pertain the adoption, the glory, the covenants, the giving of the law, the service of God, and the promises…"* In Psalm 77:8, the poet Asaph asks in his desperation, *"Has His mercy ceased forever? Has His promise failed forevermore?"* Paul answers in Romans 11:25–26a, *"For I do not desire, brethren, that you should be ignorant of this mystery, lest you should be wise in your own opinion, that blindness in part has happened to Israel until the fullness of the Gentiles has come in. And so all Israel will be saved…"* With this statement, Paul hints at that the nation of Israel will again exist.

Before I continue with the prophecies concerning Israel, let me take a look at the Jewish people. A statistic in the 1980s says that modern immorality is greatest among Protestants with 46%, among Catholics with 32%, and among the Japanese and the Jews with 1%. "Ancient ethics is about living a good and virtuous life according to the ethical virtues, that is, to become a virtuous person, while the modern notion of morality is primarily focused on the interests of other people and the idea of deontological constraints" (Gordon, n.d.). Deontological ethics "is sometimes described as responsibility, commitment, or rule-based ethics" (*Pallipedia*, n.d., "Deontological Ethics").

During my studies at the Northwest Bible College in Edmonton, Alberta, I visited a Jewish Orthodox synagogue during their worship service. Right at the entrance I was heartily welcomed. On the wall between the foyer and the worship hall was a display reading "A True Jew Is a Light and a Blessing to His Neighbourhood." The sitting order in the hall was very interesting—the men and boys sat in the centre, while the women and girls sat around the walls. This reminded me of the first Christians. Since most of them were Jews, it stands to reason that they used the same sitting order they were used to in their synagogues.

I was impressed by their honouring of the old treasurer of their congregation, who had resigned from his job due to old age. He was praised as a very gentle father who always gave love wherever he was.

It is people like this that the antisemites hate! Clearly, Satan is behind that hate.

In 1850, some Evangelical scholars discovered in the Bible that the State of Israel will be resurrected in the End Time. In about 1890, Theodor Herzl began the Movement of Zion, which demanded a national home for the Jews in Palestine. The Arabs deny to Israel the right to return to their ancient land. The truth is that there has always been a minority of Jews living there over the last two thousand years, which gives a legal right to Israel's claim to that territory. In 1917 in the Balfour declaration, a national return of the Jews to their ancient homeland was guaranteed.

Here are some Bible quotations that speak to this issue:

Isaiah 11:11–12 states,

> *It shall come to pass in that day that the Lord shall set His hand again the second time to recover the remnant of His people who are left, from Assyria and Egypt, from Pathros and Cush, from Elam and Shinar, from Hamath and the islands of the sea.*
>
> *He will set up a banner for the nations, and will assemble the outcasts of Israel, and gather together the dispersed of Judah from the four corners of the earth.*

The words *"a second time"* make it clear that this refers to a different event than when Israel returned from Assyria and Babylonia in 536 BC. The *"islands of the sea"* refer to nations that the ancients could reach only by ships. The *"four corners of the earth"* refer to North, South, East, and West—namely, the entire globe of the earth. The words *"He will set up a banner for the nations"* refer to Israel's flag with the Star of David.

Isaiah 60:8–9 makes it clear that this return belongs to our time, for the text says, *"Who are these who fly like a cloud, and like doves to their roosts? Surely the coastlands shall wait for Me; and the ships from Tarshish will come first, to bring your sons from afar…"* So the Jews will return to their ancient homeland first by ship, which happened before 1948, and later by airplanes, which is the historical fact. It still happens! The word *"Tarshish"* indicates that the ships will come from the western part of the Mediterranean Sea. This prophecy was fulfilled precisely to the order of the text! Amazing!

In Isaiah 35:1–4, God prophesies concerning the coming development of Israel's soil,

> *The wilderness and the wasteland shall be glad for them, and the desert shall rejoice and blossom as the rose; it shall blossom abundantly and rejoice, even with joy and singing. The glory of Lebanon shall be given to it, the excellence of Carmel and Sharon. They shall see the glory of the Lord, the excellency of our God.*
>
> *Strengthen the weak hands, and make firm the feeble knees. Say to those who are fearful hearted, "Be strong, do not fear! Behold, your God will come with vengeance, with the recompense of God; He will come and save you."*

In 1867, Mark Twain visited Palestine and wrote, "The further we went the hotter the sun got, and the more rocky and bare, repulsive and dreary the landscape became… There was hardly a tree or a shrub any where. Even the olive and the cactus, those fast friends of a worthless soil, had almost deserted the country…" Twain states that "Palestine is desolate and unlovely. And why should it be otherwise? Can the curse of the Deity beautify a land?" (Malul, 2018). Looking into it now, what a tremendous change has God encouraged and done!

Nowadays in the Negev desert landscape, in southern Israel, there are large horticultural farms where flowers and fruits are being produced and shipped to Europe and America. When Helen and I visited Israel in 1990, we found Israel to be a beautiful country, especially west of Jerusalem and Galilee. We felt really at home there. Thus, under our eyes, Israel has changed from a desert land to a prosperous nation! That happened by the grace of God, plus the diligence and intelligence of the Jewish people.

As Isaiah prophesied (Isaiah 66:8), so it happened: *"Who has heard such a thing? Who has seen such things? Shall the earth be made to give birth in one day? Or shall a nation be born at once? For as soon as Zion was in labor, she gave birth to her children."* That happened on May 14, 1948! The "End Time" deals mainly with the fate of Israel until the appearance of our Lord Jesus Christ for the salvation of Israel out of all its troubles.

During the Six-Day War (August 12–18, 1967), Israel conquered Old Jerusalem. According to the prophecy in Matthew 24 and Luke 21, we learn indirectly that those people who experience the capture of Old Jerusalem will face everything up to the return of Christ, who will land upon the mountain of Olives east of Jerusalem (Zechariah 14:3–4). According to Genesis 6:3, God gave man a lifespan up to 120 years. What does that mean for us?

That means that between 1967 and 2087, Jesus Christ will return to Israel. Nobody knows the exact date. The important question for you personally is, *"Will I be ready to face Him?"*

The Lord Jesus also mentioned that earthquakes will increase during the End Time (Matthew 24:7). Take a look at the graph of earthquake activity (shared with the permission of its creator at trackingbibleprophecy.org and based on data from the United States Geological Survey). Even when it comes to earthquakes, it is clear that we are in the End Time.

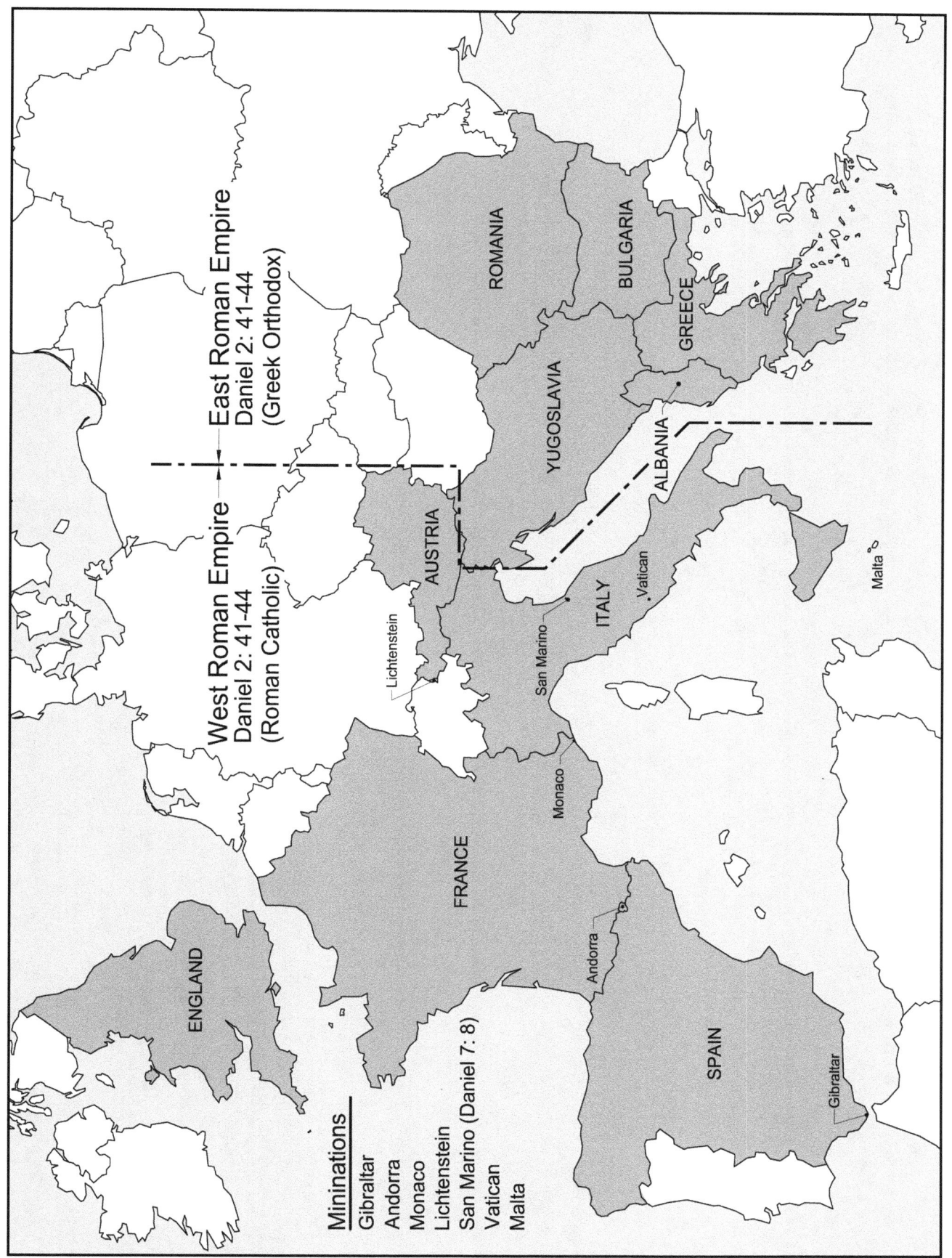

Figure 3: The Extent of Antichrist's Domain

NOTES

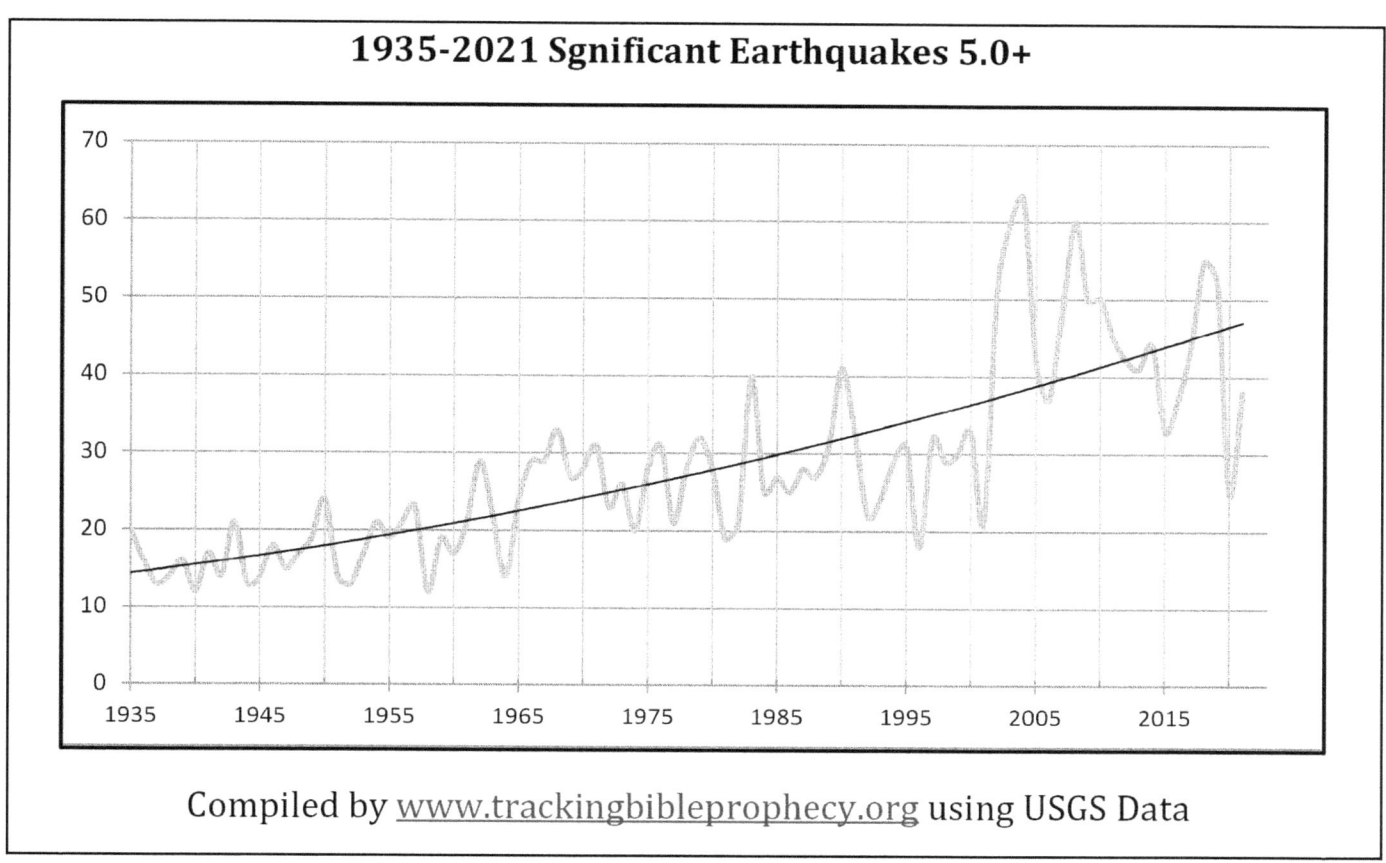

Figure 4: 1935–2021 Significant Earthquakes 5.0+

NOTES

THE SECOND SIGN OF THE END TIME AND RETURN OF JESUS CHRIST:
THE COMING OF THE ANTI-CHRISTIAN EMPIRE

THE SECOND SIGN of the End Time and return of Jesus Christ is the coming of the Anti-Christian Empire.

It is prophesied to come in Daniel chapters two and seven. Here, I will focus on chapter two. Verses 31–35 state,

> *You, O king, were watching and behold, a great image! This great image, whose splendor was excellent, stood before you; and its form was awesome. This image's head was of fine gold, its chest and arms of silver, its belly and thighs of bronze, its legs of iron, its feet partly of iron and partly of clay. You watched while a stone was cut out without hands, which struck the image on its feet of iron and clay, and broke them in pieces. Then the iron, the clay, the bronze, the silver, and the gold were crushed together, and became like chaff from the summer threshing floors; the wind carried them away so that no trace of them was found. And the stone that struck the image became a great mountain and filled the whole earth.*

According to verses 37–45 (see figure number 5), the head of gold was the Babylonian Empire, the breast and arms of silver were the Medo-Persian Empire, the bronze belly and thighs were the Greek Empire, and the two iron legs were the Roman Empire that was divided into the western Latin Empire and the eastern Byzantine Empire in 284 A.D., out of which would grow the ten nations made partly of iron and partly of potter's clay. These ten nations are represented by the toes on the feet of the statue. They grew upon Roman provincial territories, and from the western leg they are Spain, Britain (without Scotland), France, Italy, and Austria. From the eastern leg they are Greece, Bulgaria, Romania, Albania, and Yugoslavia. There are no other countries in Europe that grew up on Roman provincial territories or qualify on account of their age as children of Rome. The other countries in Europe that also exist on the territory of the former Roman Empire, like Portugal and Switzerland (breakaways from Spain and Austria), were established in the Middle Ages and have a shorter history than the ten.

The information given in Daniel chapter two is the basis for all the coming prophecies in the Bible about the Anti-Israel and Anti-Christian movement that ends with Antichrist's empire. Since there is no gap between the ten nations and the Millennium in Daniel's text to fit in a special anti-Israel and anti-Christian Empire between Daniel 2:40 and 44, *it must therefore be assumed that the ten nations form this empire.* It will be followed directly by the Millennium of Christ, the stone that became a mountain (Sicily on the map of Europe). Since this ten-nation empire will exist on a limited territory, this means that there will *not* be a world-encompassing empire, as is believed by many Evangelical scholars. The same ten nations are alluded to in Revelation 12:3; 13:1; and 17:12–14. They are clearly understood to be the Anti-Israel and Anti-Christian Empire that will be defeated by the appearance of our Lord Jesus Christ.

A lot of proponents think that the European Union will be this empire. That is not likely, considering the resistance to it which is growing in Germany and Great Britain. The German people are tired of being the financial institution that tries to redeem member nations who do not shoulder their financial responsibilities and come close to bankruptcy like Greece and Spain, while Great Britain has already left under "Brexit."

Some people maintain that Germany would also be one of the nations in the Anti-Christian Empire. That is an error. For one thing, Germany east of the Rhine River never belonged to Rome. True, the western and southern fringes were occupied by the Romans and made into provinces, and the Romans tried hard to move deeper into Germany. At one point they got as far east as the small city of Fritzlar in North Hesse, which lies about 120 km away from the Roman border, but had to withdraw on account of the strong resistance of the tribe of the Chatti. At another point, under the leadership of General Publius Quinctilius Varus, they reached the River Elbe in central Germany. According to legend, a divine woman with the name "Germania," the protecting spirit of Germany, appeared to the general on the opposite (east) side of the river, shouting across it to him, "Return, Varus; you shall not cross this river." Varus and his army turned and ended up in the battle of Teutoburger Forest (9 A.D.), where his army was totally destroyed—very few Romans escaped the forest.

He was beaten by the German Prince Hermann the Cheruscian (in Latin "Arminius") leading the German tribes of the Teutons, Chatti, and Alemanni (Westfalians, Hessians, and the Schwabs of Württemberg) into the battle with the Romans. The Romans never tried to conquer Germany again. They gave up on the conquest of Germany and instead built their famous defence wall, the "Limes Wall," from the North Sea along the Rhine River and at Regensburg following the Danube River to block the aggression of the expanding German tribes.

If you have heard Christian scholars claim that the Anti-Christian Empire will rule the whole world as we know it today, that is because they do not recognize the problems about the biblical words *"earth"* and *"all."* The earth in the view of the people living at the time when the New Testament was written encompassed mainly the coastal countries of the Mediterranean Sea, Spain, France, Italy, Albania, Macedonia, Greece, Asia Minor, Belgium, Britain; the coast of the Black Sea, especially Southern Russia; Asia up to India; and North Africa including Ethiopia. A few were aware of the "Silk Road" leading to China, and a few may have heard of Germany, Switzerland, Austria, and the Scandinavian countries. This was the biblical "whole earth" at that time. In good biblical prophecy interpretation, this fact must be taken into consideration.

The biblical word *"all"* was mostly a general term that did not mean "Everything without exception," but a part of something. There is a Greek term for this. It is called "synecdoche, a figure of speech by which whole of thing is put for part, or part for whole, i.e. *Sail* for *ship*" (Collins Canadian English Dictionary 1995).

There is only one person who will be allowed to rule the whole earth as we know it today, and that is our Lord Jesus Christ!

Proof that Antichrist will not rule the whole earth as we know it can be found in the books of Ezekiel, Zechariah, and Revelation.

In Ezekiel 38:2, we read about the leaders of the Russian Federation: Gog, Magog, the Prince of Rosh (best understood as a geographical area), and the tribes of Meshech and Tubal. In verses 5–6, members of this confederation are mentioned: *"Persia, Ethiopia, and Libya are with them, all of them with shield and helmet; Gomer and all its troops; the house of Togarmah from the far north and all its troops –many people are with you."* Apparently these nations are not subject to Antichrist's rule, but they fit into the same time frame as the Anti-Christian Empire does since their existence terminates at about the same time as Antichrist's. So both their history runs somewhat parallel.

According to the context of chapters 38 and 39, this confederation is the last force that fights against Israel and perishes there. It appears that Zechariah 14 also refers to this conflict. In Zechariah's prophecy, Antichrist's forces are no longer mentioned, but the Russian Federation is, for this battle comes after the Battle of Armageddon in which Antichrist's forces apparently were defeated by the Russian Federation and the kings of the East, after which this confederation attacks and conquers Israel—up to half of the city of Jerusalem!

The prophet Zechariah writes in chapter 14 verse 12, *"And this will be the plague with which the Lord will strike all the people who fought against Jerusalem [meaning all Israel]: their flesh shall dissolve while they stand on their feet, their eyes shall dissolve in their sockets, and their tongues shall dissolve in their mouths."* It sounds like nuclear weapons are used in this war. Revelation 14:20 says that the blood mixed with the water of Revelation 16:21 will flow as high as the horses' bridles. At this point, the Russian Federation will be defeated by the sudden appearance of Jesus Christ.

In Revelation 9:14–16, two hundred million soldiers come from the kings of the East. These soldiers must come from countries that have a big population like India and China to produce such a big army. In Revelation 16:12–16, further information is given. The kings of the East also come to fight against Antichrist and the False Prophet. This makes it clear as daylight that Antichrist has enemies, and therefore does not rule the whole world as we know it. This scenario leads up to the battle of Armageddon, a valley that lies east of the city of Haifa in Israel. Central Europe, including Poland, Hungary, Czechia, Slovakia, and Germany will be in the middle of this conflict between Russia and its allies and Antichrist's domain in Western Europe (including France and Britain), and will provide the battlefields in this conflict. In verse 16 the place of this war is revealed: *"And they gathered them together to the place called in Hebrew, Armageddon."* There, Antichrist's armies will find their demise!

Bible prophecy appears to give us three main players in the Battle of Armageddon: Antichrist, the Russian Federation, and the kings of the East. The Russians will be the victors according to Ezekiel 39. Revelation 16:14 tells us that *"the whole world"* will be involved in that battle. So will this be World War Three? It appears that some of the countries of the world are not involved in this battle as nations, but perhaps by sending soldiers to aid Antichrist against his enemies, because Ezekiel 39:6 claims that the coastlands (the lands that can only be reached beyond the sea: North and South America, Australia, and New Zealand, among others) will live in security at that time. In addition, the Lord Jesus explains in Matthew 24:38 that at that time in those countries people will be eating, drinking, marrying, and given in marriage, so apparently they will have peace in the land during the Great Tribulation period.

According to the prophecy in Daniel chapter two, God is in full control of this event. Daniel 2:31–34 states,

> *You, O king, were watching; and behold, a great image! This great image, whose splendor was excellent, stood before you; and its form was awesome. This image's head was of fine gold, its chest and arms of silver, its belly and thighs of bronze, its legs of iron, its feet partly of iron and partly of clay. You watched while a stone was cut out without hands, which struck the image on its feet of iron and clay, and broke them in pieces.*

Verse 35, *"...the stone that struck the image became a great mountain and filled the whole earth,"* refers to the destruction of the Anti-Christian Empire consisting of 10 nations, and it is illustrated on the map of Europe by the island Sicily (the stone) hitting the toe of the Italian boot, the centre of the Anti-Christian Empire. The stone becoming a mountain and filling the earth relates to the growth of the Kingdom of God, which will be victorious over Antichrist and his empire and fill the entire earth in the Millennium.

Notes

In the following chapters we will hear more of the main players of the End Time story, especially in the book of Revelation. They are eight: Israel, Christianity, Antichrist, the two witnesses, the false prophet, the Great Harlot, Satan, and the Lord Jesus Christ.

Many proponents believe that the book of Revelation runs chronologically. That is an error, as seen in stories of the return of the Lord Jesus Christ, of which there are six direct and indirect reports: Revelation 6:16–17; 10:7; 11:15; 14:1; 14:14; and 19:11–16. All these reports of Christ's return occur at the time of the end of things during the Great Tribulation story.

Furthermore, the treaty of Israel with Antichrist begins in Revelation chapter six and ends in chapter nineteen. The seven seals reveal the things that happen during the seven years of the treaty of Israel with Antichrist according to Daniel 9:27. The seven trumpets are actually battle signals of the war of God against Antichrist, that begins with the erection of Antichrist's image in the temple of Jerusalem three and a half years into this treaty and begins the Great Tribulation proper, also called "Jacob's Trouble." This causes a great rebellion in Israel, including the assassination of Antichrist (Revelation 13:3), in which many Jews will perish. The seven bowls of wrath begin at the fifth seal in response to the martyrs' plead for God's action.

The duration of the treaty of Israel with Antichrist looks like this (see also figure 15): the seven seals in seven years (chapters 6–8); at the midpoint of their cycle, the 3.5 year mark, the seven battle signals will begin (chapters 8–11), and then at the fifth seal or fifth year, the seven bowls of wrath will begin (chapter 16). The three series of seven will take different amounts of time, but *all three will conclude together at the coming of the Lord Jesus Christ*.

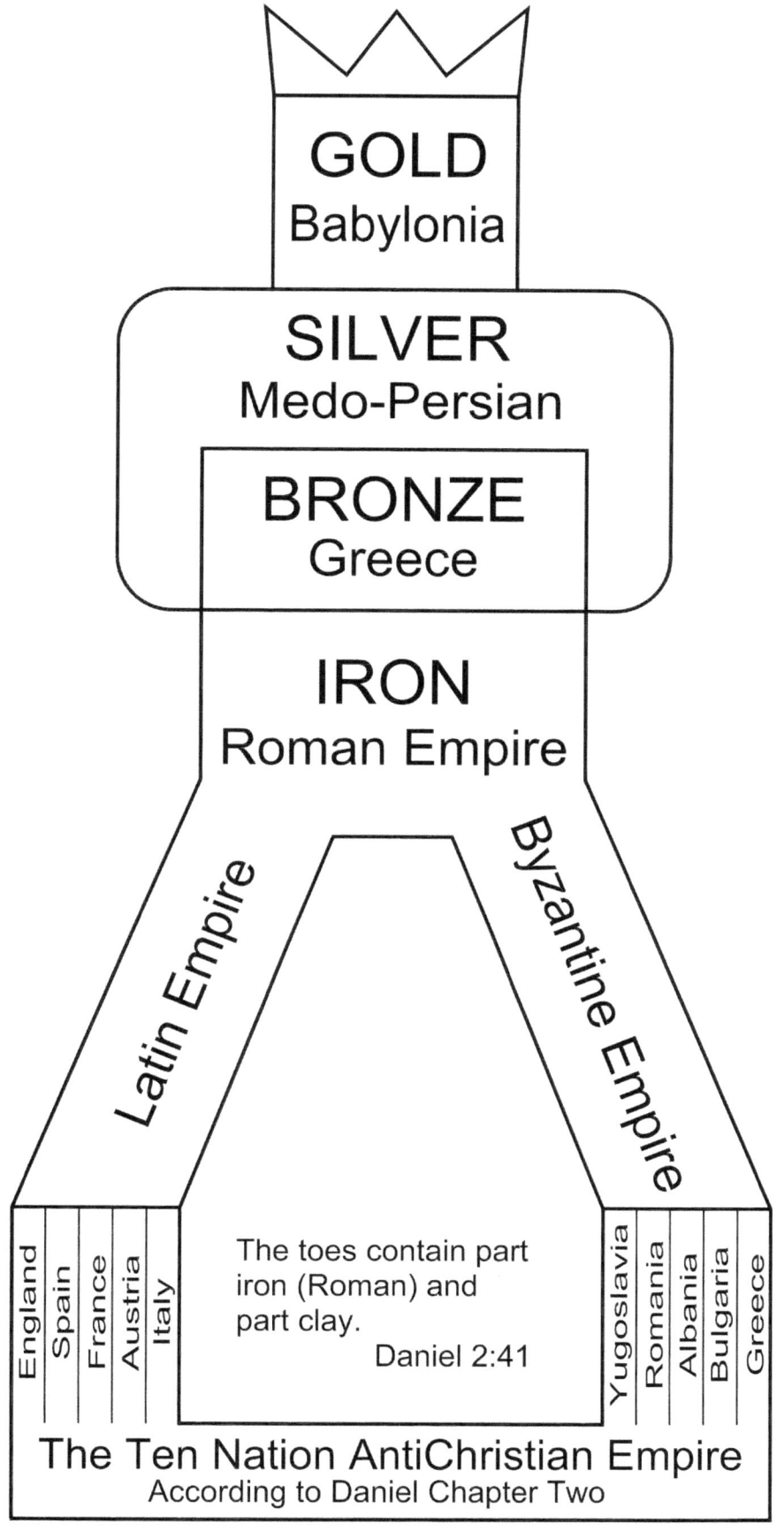

Figure 5: The Great Image of Nebuchadnezzar

NOTES

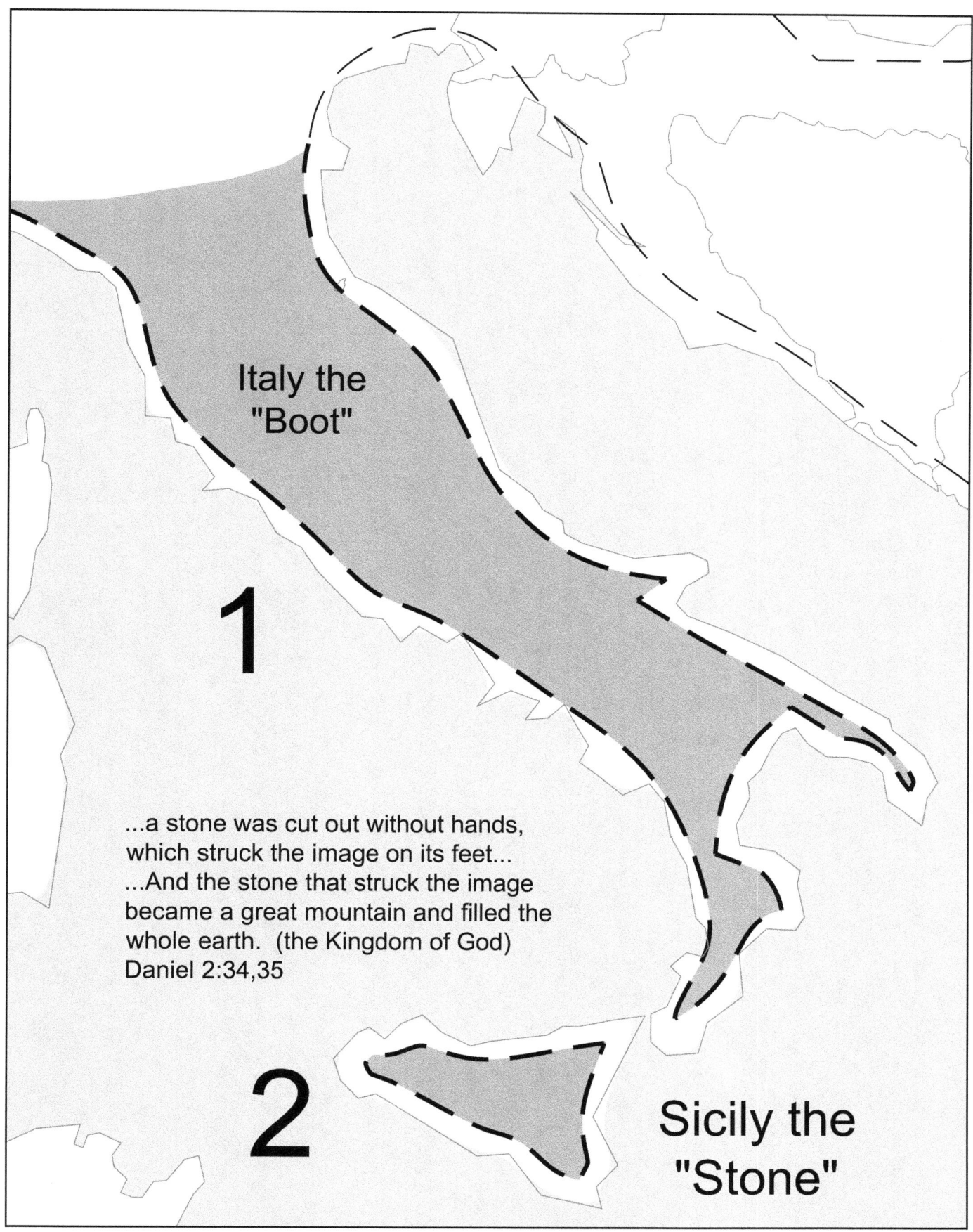

Figure 6: Italy—The Centre of Antichrist's Empire

NOTES

THE THIRD SIGN OF THE END TIME AND RETURN OF JESUS CHRIST:
FINDING THE REAL ANTICHRIST

TO CHRISTIANS, ANTICHRIST is "Antichrist." To Jews, he is called "Antimessiah." The term "messiah" means "the anointed one" in Hebrew, while the title "Christ" is a Greek rendering of the same idea.

"*Little children, it is the last hour; and as you have heard that the Antichrist is coming, even now many antichrists have come, by which we know that it is the last hour.*" Thus the Apostle John wrote at the end of the first century (1 John 2:18). Apparently he believed that the real Antichrist was coming very soon. He also added that many antichrists have come.

To this we can say "Amen," for this happens in our age as well. The London Telegraph reports that their office is visited often by someone who claims that he/she is the Christ or Messiah, requesting that they please print their message to the world. Recently, on the Dr. Phil Show, the good doctor interviewed a man who claims to be the Christ.

Antichrist's Name and Physical Features

One thing is for certain: over the centuries, people—Christians and Jews alike—have been looking for Antichrist. Someone found out that if you use matches to spell "Stalin," you can move them around to spell "666," the numerical value of Antichrist's name (Revelation 13:18), so is Stalin the real Antichrist? No!

People have tried to fix this title on German emperors and American presidents, Hitler and Mussolini, and many others. Martin Luther is credited for determining that the Roman Catholic Pope seems to qualify for the Antichrist because the words of his title on his crown are *Vicarius filii Dei*, which give us in Roman numerals the sum of 666. This is nice, but sorry, the Pope cannot fill the boots of Antichrist, because we are not looking for the numerical value of his title, but of his name. But as we will find out later, he might be able to qualify as the False Prophet, the partner of Antichrist.

In the second century, the bishop Irenaeus wrote that the letters in the Greek word *Lateinos* add up to 666 in Greek letter values, which may indicate that Antichrist is going to be an Italian man. Many have tried to puzzle this out and have come to false results. The solution to this puzzle lies in the question: "In which language are we to find the solution to this problem?" The answer is actually very simple. One must look to find the answer in the Hebrew language, because the Great Tribulation mainly affects Israel. In Hebrew the number 666 is represented by the following letters: Taw=400; Resh=200; Samekh=60; and Waw=6. These four letters add up to 666. The letters read with the vowels inserted: Thera Sawa. That appears to be Antichrist's name.

The ancient Church Fathers contributed to finding the real Antichrist. Here is a word of Origen, who is one of the best learned among the Church Fathers: "The Antichrist is the son of Satan." He can say that based on Genesis 3:15, where God says, *"And I will put enmity between you and the woman, and between your seed and her Seed; He shall bruise your head, and you shall bruise His heel."* The observant reader will notice that in the case of Satan's seed the father is mentioned, and in the case of the woman's seed the mother is mentioned—the Virgin Mary, who gave birth to our Lord Jesus. So Antichrist is indeed the son of Satan.

Some ancient Church Fathers claim that Antichrist shall be born of a demon-possessed virgin, in contrast to the Virgin Mary, who was possessed by the Holy Spirit. This being the case, Antichrist would be born a Nephilim like those in Genesis chapter six and 1 Samuel 17:49–51, as well as 2 Samuel 21:16, 18–20. They were all giants, and verse 20 states that they had six fingers on each hand and six toes on each foot. This feature can be seen on the map of Europe when looking upon the province of Achaia of Greece. This characteristic still exists among some Palestinian families. That there really were some giants on the earth in ancient times is confirmed lately by archaeological findings. Their size was about three metres. Reverend Johann Joseph Gaßner (1727–1779) writes: "According to several saints, Antichrist will be born of parents involved with magic and will become the most renowned magician, doing outstanding miracles."

This research leads me to say that *we have found the real Antichrist*. His name is Thera Sawa, and you will recognize him by his great statue and having six fingers on each hand and six toes on each foot. It is possible that he already exists, because we already live in the end times.

He will be born in Bethlehem, be half Jewish and half Palestinian, and claim to be a descendant of David. He must be able to prove this in the presence of the Jewish people. This is humanly possible, because the family of David is known during history right into the eighteenth century A.D. After that, the family went into hiding, probably into the United States. However, some Jewish priests know where they are today.

Antichrist will copy Christ, even to the point of experiencing a resurrection from the dead (Revelation 13:3). Paul writes about Antichrist in 2 Thessalonians 2:3–4: *"Let no one deceive you by any means; for that Day [the return of Christ] will not come unless the falling away comes first, and the man of sin is revealed, the son of perdition who opposes and exalts himself above all that is called God or that is worshiped, so that he sits as God in the temple of God, showing himself that he is God."*

Antichrist's Career

In the Bible, a ruler and his domain are often seen as one unit. So it is also with Antichrist. Antichrist and his original domain are called *"a little horn"* in Daniel 7:8–11, 20–26. According to this text, Antichrist will speak pompous words, make war against the saints, and win that war. He will be different from the first kingdoms. He shall subdue three kings (rebuilding the fractured Yugoslavian nation), and speak pompous words against the Most High. He shall wear out the saints of the Most High, and shall attempt to change times and law. Then the saints shall be given into his hands for three and a half years, after which his dominion shall be taken away from him and be destroyed forever, and the greatness of all nations under the whole heaven (that is, the whole world as we know it!) shall be given to God's people within an everlasting kingdom.

According to Daniel 9:27, Antichrist shall enter into a seven-year treaty with Israel. According to the Church Father Hippolytus (170–235 A.D.), Antichrist will have the temple in Jerusalem rebuilt. It will be built north of the Dome of the Rock upon the foundation of the second temple, which has been located there. Three and a half years into this treaty, he suddenly will erect a speaking image of himself in the temple (Matthew 24:15; 2

Thessalonians 2:4). This will cause a furious rebellion of the Jews, who will be very angry about Antichrist's act of temple desecration.

Some of them will be successful in assassinating him. With the help of modern medicine, he will be brought back to life according to Revelation 13:3, 12. From this point onward, he will fight the rebellious Jews and incarcerate and kill many of them, as well as Christians who support Israel (Revelation 6:9–11). Because of his assassination, he will lose his right eye and one arm will be crippled (Zechariah 11:17). On the map of Europe, this is illustrated by the Black Sea that shows no feature of an eye and the peninsula of Chalcidice (Chalkidiki) of Greece. God will also act upon this abomination of desolation done by Antichrist and begin the war of the seven trumpets (battle signals).

Now let us find the territory that he will rule.

Like Antichrist, it is called the "Little Horn." If all the other horns in this prophecy are nations, the Little Horn must be a miniature nation (microstate). I checked the territory of the former Byzantine Empire, and no miniature nations exist within it. I also checked the territory of the former Latin Empire and behold, there are seven mini-nations. From west to east, they are Gibraltar, Andorra, Monaco, Lichtenstein, Vatican, Malta, and San Marino. Checking their age (the Little Horn must grow up from within the Roman Empire according to Daniel 7:8, 20–22), only San Marino qualifies. True to the text that says that it is to be ruled differently than all the others, San Marino is ruled by two Capitani Reggenti. According to legend, it was founded by a Dalmatian stone cutter named Marinus in 301 A.D., and existed for 175 years within the decaying Roman Empire. So it fulfills the exact requirements of the text in Daniel 7:8! San Marino is the oldest continually existing republic in the world. The border of San Marino looks like a head with a face and a little horn on top facing east on the map. (The Danish peninsula of Jutland also looks like a man's face, and it represents Antichrist being attacked by the Lion of the North, Scandinavia. It is labelled as number four on Figure 16, "Scandinavia: The Lion of Judah." See also Figure 2. As I explained earlier, I believe there are two images of the Antichrist on the map of Europe because Jutland represents Antichrist as a powerful politician and shows Christ attacking him, while the face on San Marino's border represents Antichrist as a small political power before his assassination.) The coat of arms of San Marino is of great interest. It shows three towers standing on three hilltops wearing feathers. If you turn this picture upside down, you get an inverted 666!

San Marino mainly occupies the slopes and summit of a mountain named "Monte Titano." This name translates into English as "Mountain of the Giant," which by God's design hints at the Nephilim. The Jewish history writer Josephus writes that the Nephilim of Genesis six were the product of demons who assumed a human body and had sex with women. These men were giants, very strong, evil, and brutal, and they had a lower intelligence than normal people. According to certain theologians, such persons are to appear again in the end time. The evangelist Emil Meyer (1948) reported that he had met one hundred women who complained that during the night they were sexually molested by men who came to them through locked doors. He claims that he could set ninety-nine of them free from these demons.

San Marino also traditionally maintains a close relationship with the Pope. What has San Marino to do with Antichrist? Well, he will become a citizen of it and use it as a pedestal to get into European politics! This is how our God is in control of end time events.

In Revelation 19:20 we read about the end of Antichrist and his prophet, *"Then the beast [another name for Antichrist because of his brutality] was captured, and with him the false prophet who worked signs in his presence, by which he deceived those who received the mark of the beast and those who worshiped his image. These two were cast alive into the lake of fire burning with brimstone."* That is the end of Antichrist and his false prophet.

NOTES

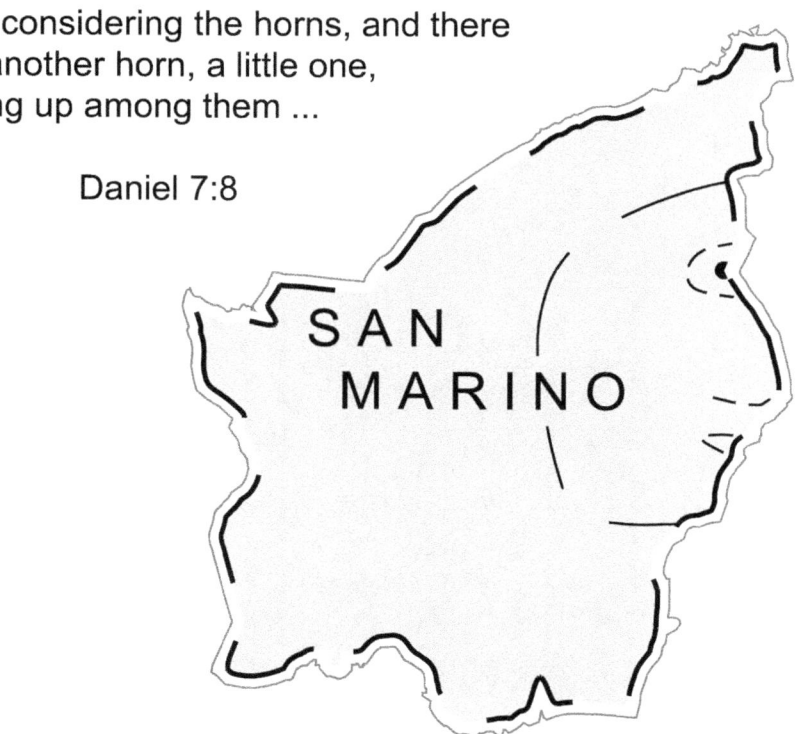

> I was considering the horns, and there was another horn, a little one, coming up among them ...
>
> Daniel 7:8

The ministate of San Marino illustrates the Antichrist before his assassination

> ... And there, in this horn, were eyes like the eyes of a man, and a mouth speaking pompous words.
>
> Daniel 7:8

Figure 7: San Marino – The Antichrist Before His Assassination

NOTES

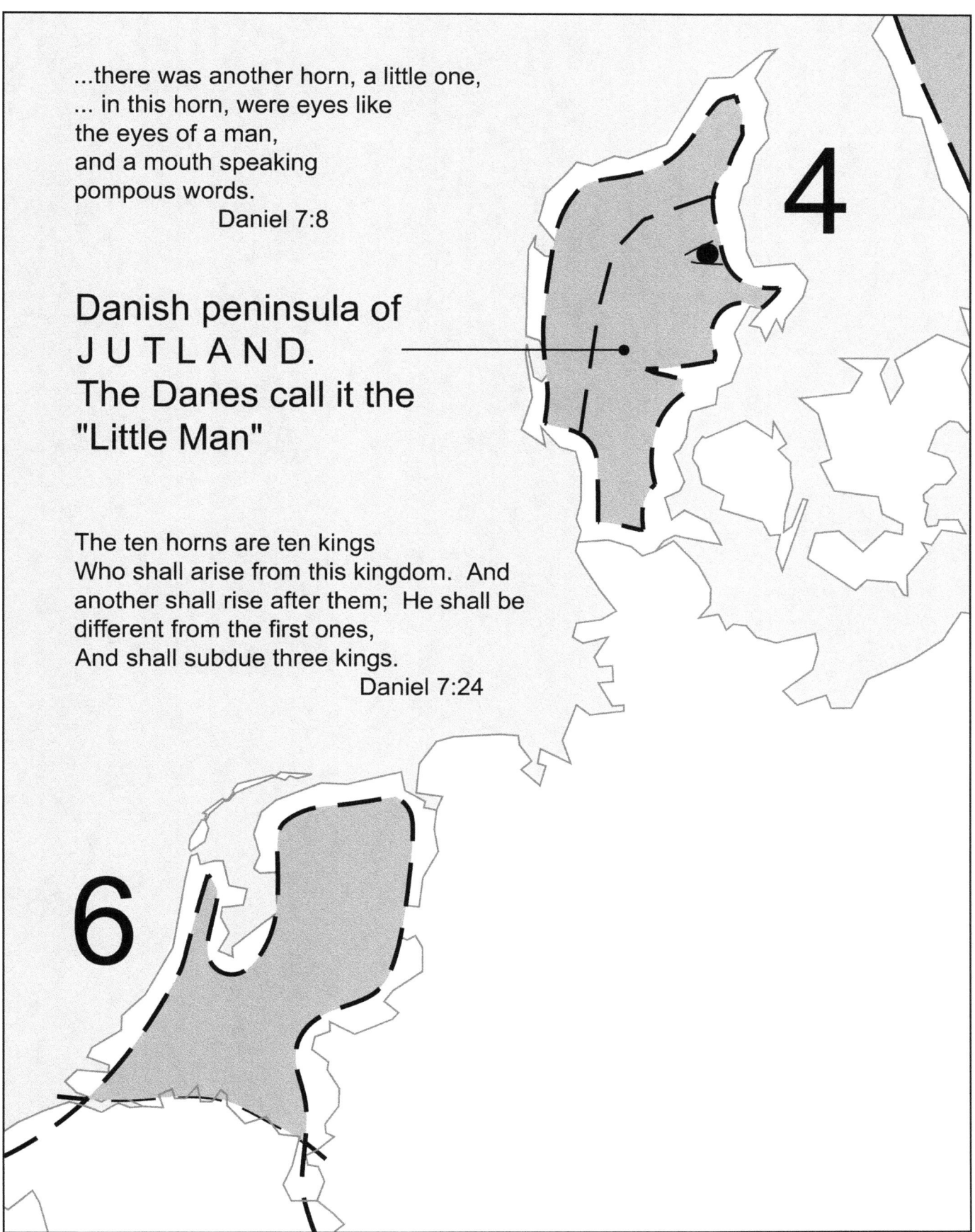

Figure 8: Jutland – The Antichrist After His Assassination

NOTES

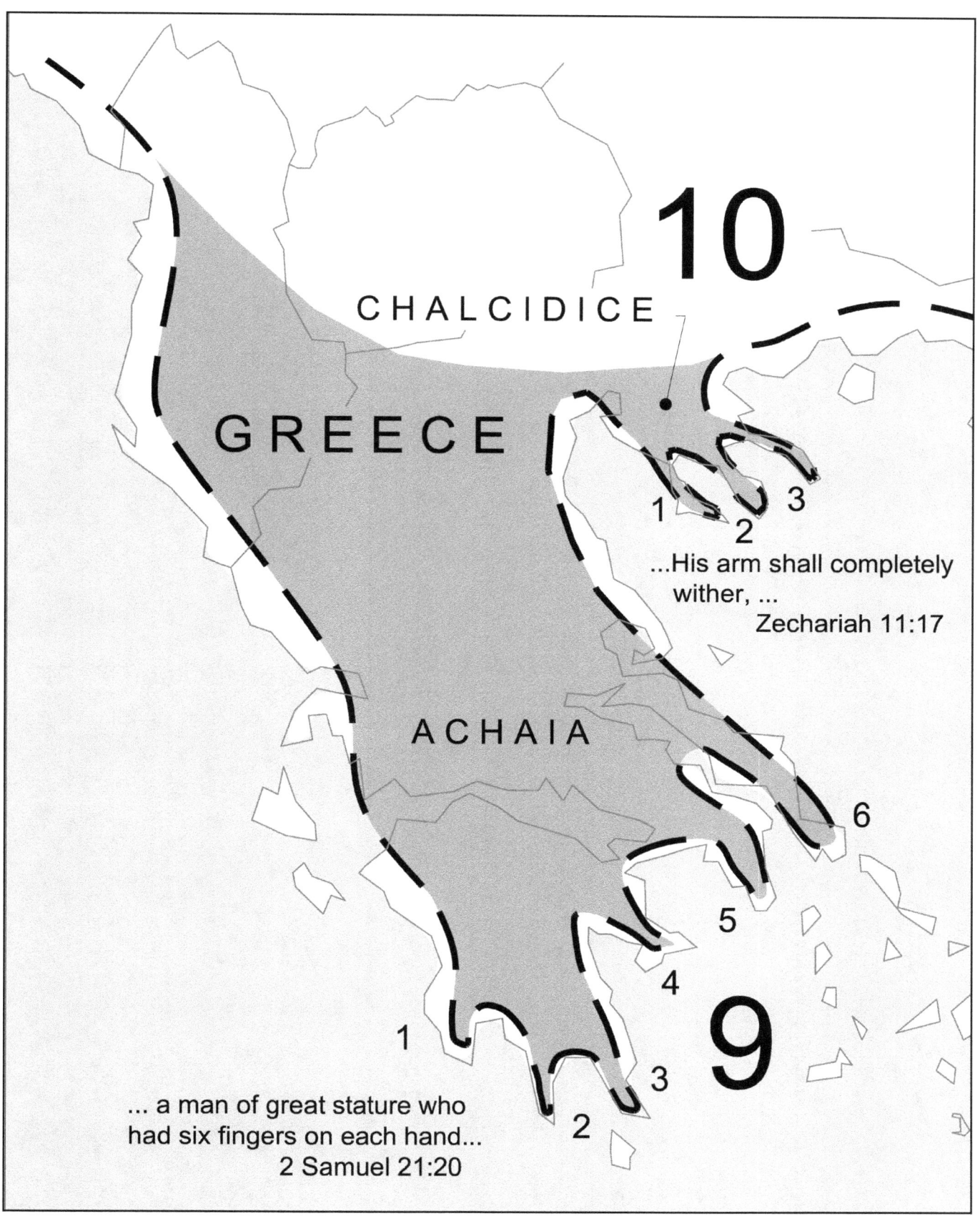

Figure 9: Greece – Six Toes and Crippled Arm

NOTES

The Coat of Arms of San Marino

His number (of the letters of his name) shall be 666 in Hebrew

(תרסן = Thera Sawa)

Turn this Coat of Arms upside down and you get an inverted 666

Figure 10: Coat of Arms of San Marino
(Image source: https://en.wikipedia.org/wiki/Coat_of_arms_of_San_Marino (public domain))

NOTES

THE FOURTH SIGN OF THE END TIME AND RETURN OF JESUS CHRIST:
FINDING THE FALSE PROPHET

I SEARCHED ON Google for false prophets, and I was overwhelmed to find so many that I quit looking. Yes, there are the old standbys, like Joseph Smith and Charles Taze Russell. Add to them the mass of liberal theologians of the nineteenth and twentieth centuries, as well as the prosperity preachers of the twentieth and twenty-first centuries, and you got more than your fill. Yet somewhere among them, there exists the False Prophet of Revelation chapters thirteen, seventeen, and eighteen!

In the Bible we will begin with Revelation chapter thirteen. Here is the text:

> *Then I saw another beast coming out of the earth, and he had two horns like a lamb and spoke like a dragon. And he exercises all the authority of the first beast in his presence, and causes the earth and those who dwell in it to worship the beast, whose deadly wound was healed. He performs great signs, so that he even makes fire come down from heaven on the earth in the sight of men. And he deceives those who dwell on the earth by those signs which he was granted to do in the sight of the beast, telling those who dwell on the earth to make an image to the beast who was wounded by the sword and lived. He was granted to give breath to the image of the beast, that the image of the beast should both speak and cause as many as would not worship the image of the beast to be killed. He causes all, both small and great, rich and poor, free and slave, to receive a mark on their right hand or on their foreheads, and that no one may buy or sell except one who has the mark or the name of the beast, or the number of his name.*
>
> *Here is wisdom. Let him who has understanding calculate the number of the beast, for it is the number of a man: His number is 666.* (v. 11–18)

It is generally assumed that the lamb with two horns represents a religious identity that split into two factions (the two horns). It is thought that this represents the Catholic Church that split into the Roman Catholic and Greek Orthodox Church in 1054 A.D. There have been meetings held between them to find a possibility for unification; however, so far they have not been very successful. The Polish archbishop Jeremiasz is of the opinion that unification attempts should be continued. However, at this present time, a number of Ukrainian Catholic churches have entered into a special relationship with Rome which allows them to keep their Eastern Orthodox rituals and have their priests marry women.

These are the things the False Prophet will do:

1. Exercise all the authority of Antichrist.
2. Cause the people on the earth to worship Antichrist.
3. Perform great miracles, even making fire come down from heaven.
4. Deceive the people on the earth.
5. Tell people living on the earth to make an image of Antichrist.
6. Give this image the ability to speak.
7. Cause the people who do not worship Antichrist to be killed.
8. Cause all people to wear a sign on the right hand or the forehead.
9. This sign will be the name or the numerical number of the name of Antichrist, which is 666.
10. Permit no one to buy or sell unless he/she wears this sign of Antichrist on his/her right hand or forehead.

Since the script on the crown of the pope contains the number 666 found in the words *Vicarius Filii Dei,* he is very much a candidate for the False Prophet's position.

The False Prophet is the head of the religious organisation called the "Great Harlot" in Revelation chapters seventeen and eighteen. This church is called a "harlot" in contrast to the "virgin" churches in Matthew chapter twenty-five, because it has added doctrines that are not biblical, and it has been involved with secular governments. On the map of Europe, she is represented by England as her head. The golden cup in her hand is found along the border of France with Germany and Switzerland, which gives the outline of half a chalice. If you fold it over, you see the full cup of the Great Harlot.

She is shown in the Bible to sit on a scarlet beast with seven heads and ten horns. This beast is the same political unit as the one in Revelation chapters twelve and thirteen, the "dragon" who persecutes Israel and her Christian friends. The Great Harlot is said to sit on many waters, which are many nations. This indicates that she is a religious world power. She has influence on the kings of the earth (the rulers of the ten kingdoms). It is known that the Roman Catholic Church has this influence on those ten kingdoms.

Revelation 17:4 indicates that this church has both ecclesiastical and secular powers in the colours *"purple and scarlet."* The *"precious stones and pearls"* refer to the treasures she owns. The *"golden cup"* points to the golden communion cup the pope uses in his services. The *"abominations and the filthiness of her fornication"* hint at her false doctrines—for example, the release of sins by paying money to her and the worship of saints, especially of Mary, the mother of Jesus. *"Her fornication"* points also to the sexual misdeeds occurring among her clergy as well in some of her convents, for example, "NEW STATS: 10% of Catholic priests were pedophiles and still counting, 20 to 200 times more than general population" https://www.bishop-accountability.org/2021/03/are-catholic-clergy-more-likely-to-be-paedophiles-than-the-general-public-redux/ and https://cityofangels8.blogspot.com/2010/09/new-stats-10-percent-of-catholic.html. The *"blood of the saints and the blood of the martyrs of Jesus"* (v. 6) refers to the sixty million non-Catholic Christians she has murdered during the past centuries, as well as during the Great Tribulation period.

Because of God's threat to punish this church, the Evangelical believers in her fold are called to exit from that church in Revelation 18:4–6: *"Come out of her, my people, lest you share in her sins, and lest you receive of her plagues. For her sins have reached to heaven, and God has remembered her iniquities. Render to her just as she rendered to you, and repay her double according to her works; in the cup which she has mixed, mix double for her."*

In verse 9 of chapter 17, seven mountains are mentioned. It is a fact that the city of Rome sits on seven mountains. According to verse 16, the rulers of the ten nations hate this harlot even though they act with false respect to her at the present time. Chapter 18 is a song that goes in details concerning the destruction of this church, which shall come upon her *"in one day"* according to verse 8. That day is the same one as when Christ appears to save Israel out of Russia's clutches, according to the prophet Zechariah (14:1–7):

> *Behold, the day of the Lord is coming, and your spoil will be divided in your midst. For I will gather all the nations to battle against Jerusalem; the city shall be taken, the houses rifled, and the women ravished. Half of the city shall go into captivity, but the remnant of the people shall not be cut off from the city.*
>
> *Then the Lord will go forth and fight against those nations, as He fights in the day of battle. And in that day His feet will stand on the Mount of Olives, which faces Jerusalem on the east. And the Mount of Olives shall be split in two, from east to west, making a very large valley; half of the mountain shall move toward the north and half of it toward the south.*
>
> *Then you shall flee through my mountain valley, for the mountain valley shall reach to Azal. Yes, you shall flee as you fled from the earthquake in the days of Uzziah king of Judah.*
>
> *Thus the Lord my God will come, and all the saints with you.*
>
> *It shall come to pass in that day that there will be no light; the lights will diminish. It shall be one day which is known to the Lord—neither day nor night. But at evening time it shall happen that it will be light.*

This happens at Jerusalem, and at the same time the destruction of the Harlot Church happens in Rome.

NOTES

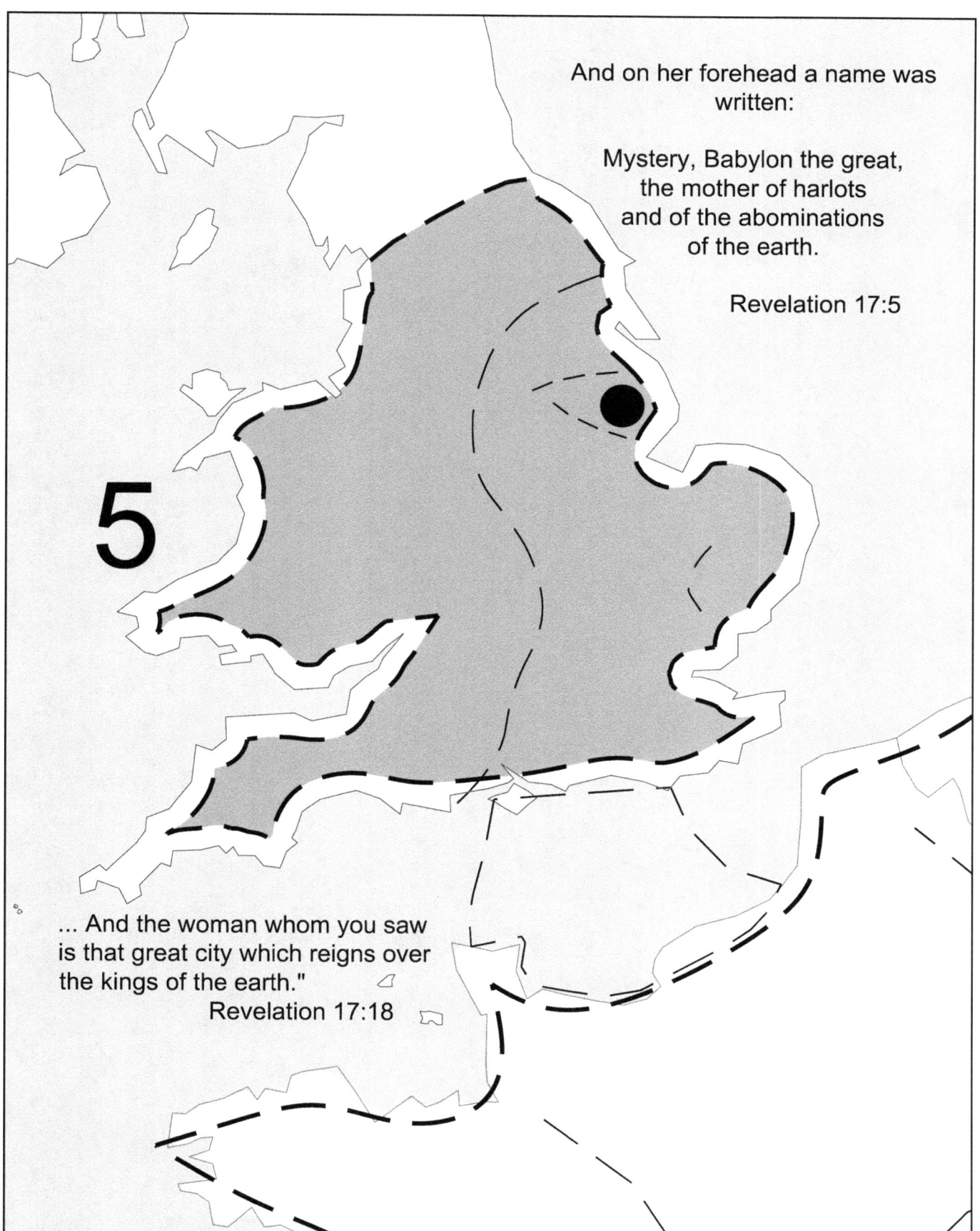

Figure 11: England – The Head of the "Great Harlot"

NOTES

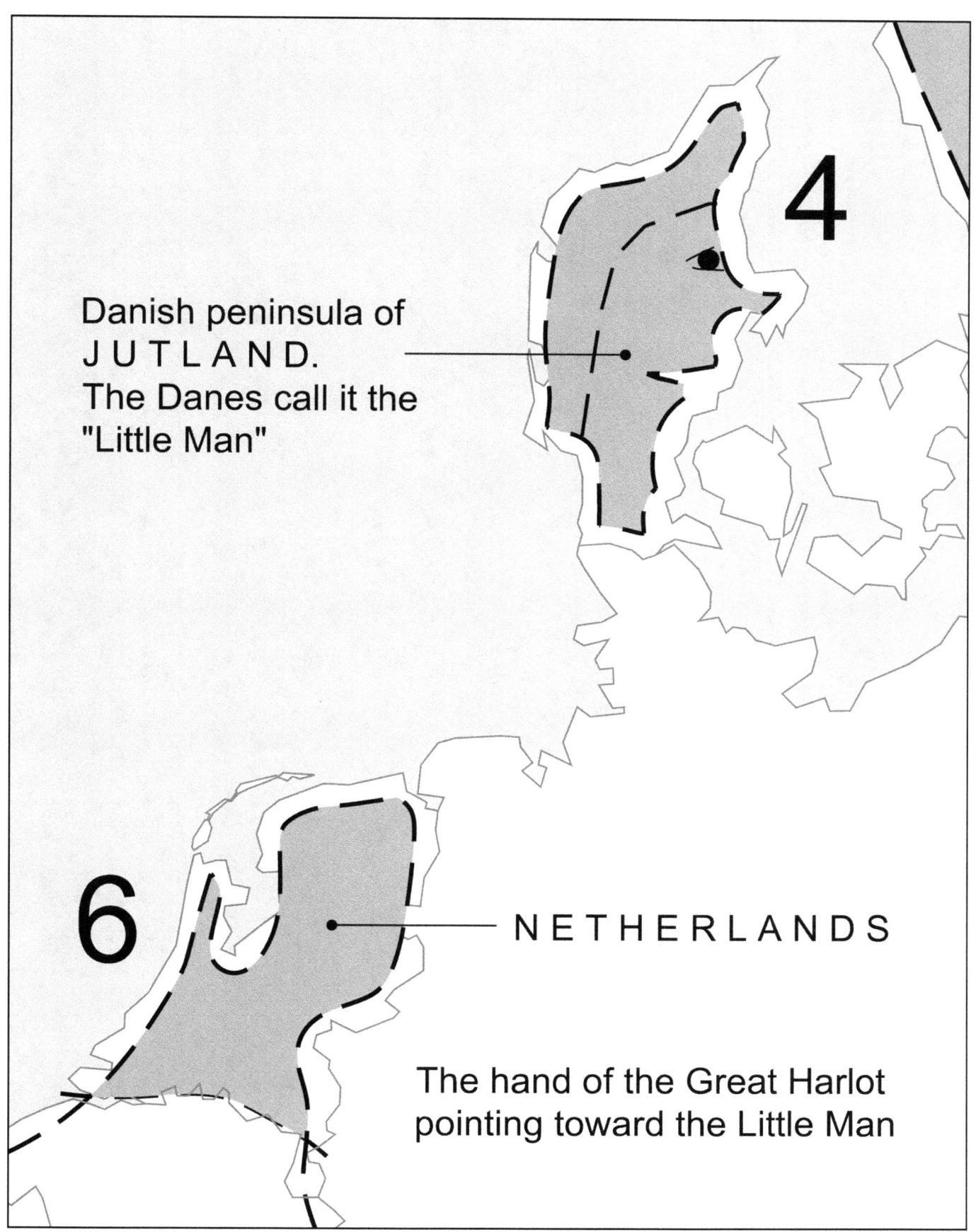

Figure 12: Netherlands – The Hand of the "Great Harlot"

NOTES

FINDING THE FALSE PROPHET

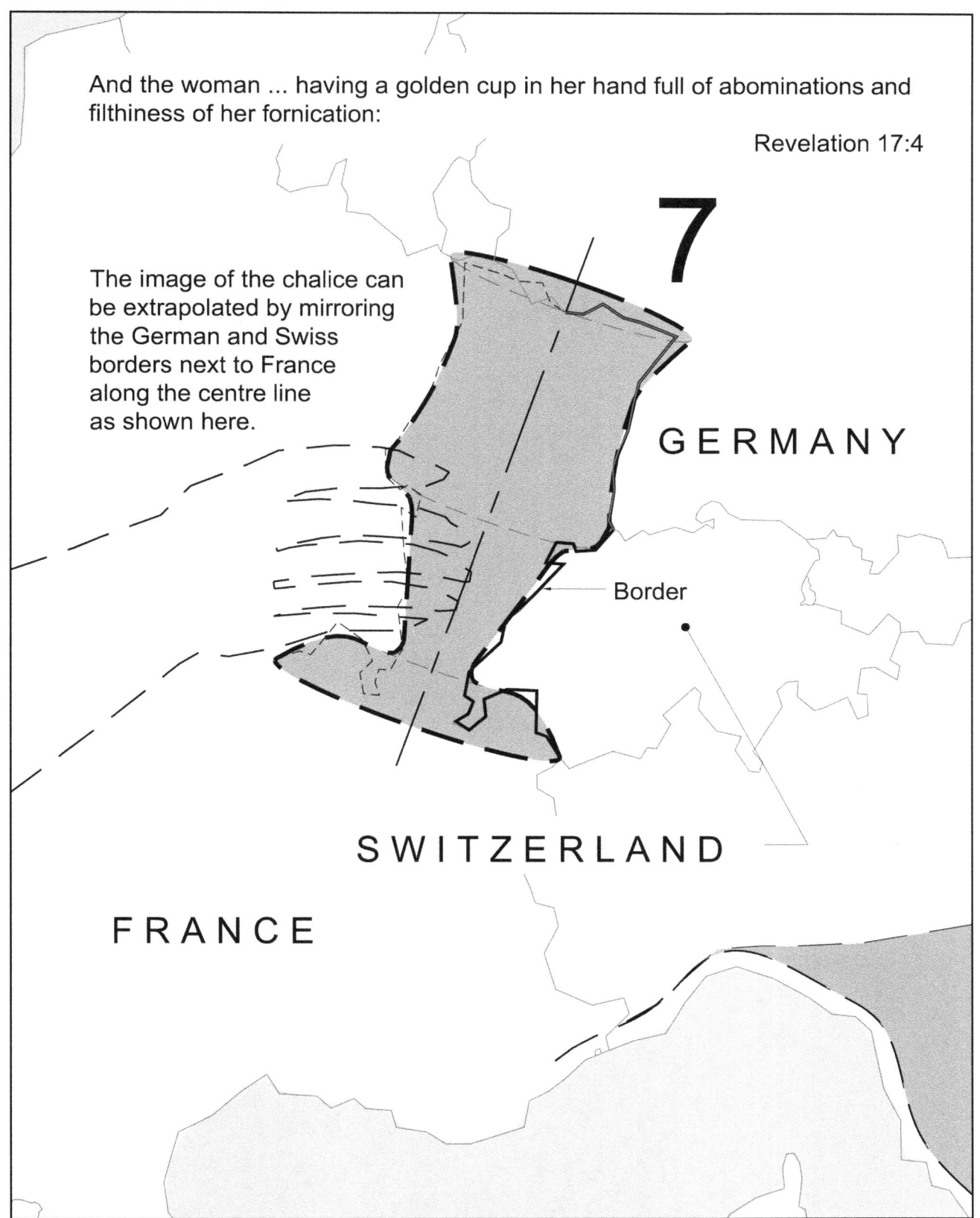

Figure 13: The Golden Cup

In the other hand of the Great Harlot is illustrated by the French border with Germany and Switzerland looking like the lines of half a chalice. Fold it over symmetrically and you see the full cup.

NOTES

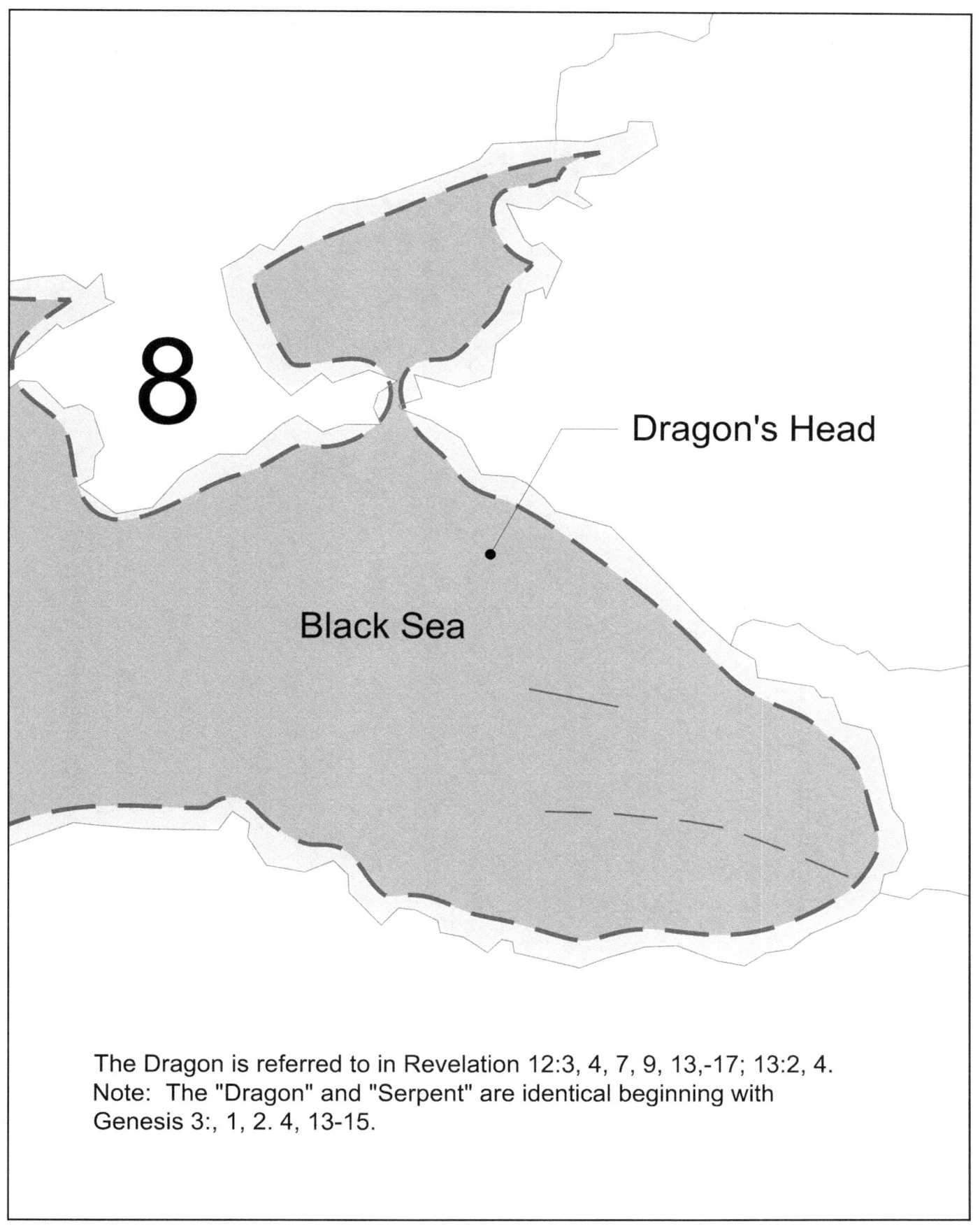

Figure 14: The Black Sea – The "Dragon's Head"

NOTES

THE FIFTH SIGN OF THE END TIME AND RETURN OF JESUS CHRIST:
THE GREAT FALLING AWAY

PAUL WRITES IN 2 Thessalonians 2:3, *"Let no one deceive you by any means; for that Day [the return of Christ] will not come unless the falling away comes first, and the man of sin is revealed, the son of perdition…"* The Great Falling Away will come before the time of Antichrist and find its fullness in Antichrist. The words *"the falling away comes first, and the man of sin is revealed"* seems to hint at the fact that Christians will still be on earth and see Antichrist. Today, this movement away from biblical Christianity is already in full swing.

According to many Protestants, the Great Apostasy began with Emperor Constantine the Great (325 A.D.). They accuse him of having merged paganism with Christianity. This had a corrupting effect on beliefs of the Church, and through centuries of succession by poor, often politically motivated church leadership, abuses of scripture became prevalent. Doctrines were invented that had no scriptural basis; for instance, that salvation comes by subjecting oneself to the seven sacraments of the Church. Another false doctrine was the belief that paying money for the departed would get them out of hell, as propagated by the Friar Johann Tetzel (1465-1519). However, most traditional Christians agree that the biblical message itself was never ultimately lost to mankind.

Then began the rise of the *"Enlightenment,"* from about 1450 A.D. Among the leaders was the scholar Desiderius Roterodamus Erasmus, who is called the "Prince of the Humanists." Some scholars began to believe in "Natural Religion" and Deism, and rejected the authority of the Bible. They disavowed faith in any revealed religion or interaction of the Creator with His creation. As time went on, they rejected traditional teachings about the virgin birth and the resurrection of Jesus Christ. They viewed the Bible not as a collection of factual statements, and they revived the allegorical interpretation of the Bible. Out of this movement grew modern "Liberal Theology."

One of their leaders was the liberal scholar Friedrich Daniel Ernst Schleiermacher (1768–1834). He disassociated himself from believing in Jesus Christ as the Saviour of the world, and began the "Higher Criticism" of the Bible which finally tore it to shreds, a book not worthy of believing in, so that only its covers remained intact. Because of this he is called the Father of Modern Liberal Theology. This trend of religious thought continued unabated throughout the nineteenth and twentieth centuries. It produced such liberal scholars as Rudolph Bultmann (1884–1976), Paul Tillich (1886–1965), and Charles Augustus Briggs (1841–1913).

The main reason that this teaching came about lies in the fact that parents who could afford to send their sons to the university to become pastors did not encourage their sons to cultivate a personal relationship with God by accepting the Lord Jesus Christ as their Saviour and Lord. They just wanted to give their sons an easier lifestyle. So these unconverted men began to doubt the authority of the Bible and were led by Satan to reject the traditional Christian beliefs in the virgin birth, the miracles of Jesus, and His resurrection from the dead. When their teachings became the common fare of the uneducated, it had the effect of destroying the simple faith of the masses, who consequently marched out of the churches. So the "Great Falling Away" has come into full bloom.

It has gotten so bad that most Lutheran clergy identify with this evil trend, so that conservative pastors in the Lutheran church are made to look like outcasts. For example, the pastor of a great church in Bremen has come under censure by the leadership of the city because he does not associate himself with being "politically correct." The general public is so estranged from biblical morality and teaching that it sounds strange to them when a pastor calls homosexuality a sin and preaches the traditional Gospel. They would like to silence him.

As a result, Germany and other formerly Protestant countries like the Scandinavian countries and the Netherlands, all of which used to send missionaries to Africa and Asia, have become the modern mission field themselves for Evangelicals in America and Africa.

This Anti-Christian trend will grow until the Antichrist himself appears on the political scene of European politics.

THE SIXTH SIGN OF THE END TIME AND RETURN OF JESUS CHRIST:
THE QUICK SPREAD OF BIBLICAL CHRISTIANITY IN THE WORLD

AMONG ALL THE negative occurrences in the world today, there is a positive trend, at least for us as Bible-oriented Christians: the quick spread of biblical Christianity in the world.

In Matthew 24:14, the Lord Jesus says, *"…this gospel of the kingdom will be preached in all the entire world as a witness to all the nations, and then the end will come."*

Observe, not everybody who hears the gospel will accept it, though many will. What you never, or very rarely, hear from the news media that are controlled by atheists and humanists is how fast biblical Christianity is progressing in the world. You are rather made to believe that Christianity is abating in the world.

According to statistics, there is less than a 1% minority of true Evangelical Christians left in Germany who live according to the gospel message (Johnson, 2012). Things are similar in other former Protestant countries in Europe. In the United States, out of every ten teenagers only three still visit worship services. In Canada supposedly 10% are true Evangelicals. The percentage is growing because of the mass immigration of Christians from Muslim countries; otherwise, the religious situation would be similar to the European countries.

Revelation 14:6–7 reads,

> *Then I saw another angel flying in the midst of heaven, having the everlasting gospel to preach to those who dwell on the earth- to every nation, tribe and people—saying with a loud voice, "Fear God and give glory to Him, for the hour of His judgment has come; and worship Him who made heaven and earth, the sea and springs of water."*

One such angel was Dr. Billy Graham, who led millions to accept Jesus Christ as their Saviour and Lord around the whole world. The word "Angel" also means "Servant," and this sense of the word is used in Revelation chapters two and three in the letters to the seven churches. You can include as angels also workers in the International United Bible Societies as well as those who create Christian media productions on TV and radio.

According to Wycliffe, there are 7,378 spoken languages in the world. As of 2022, the Bible has been translated into many languages from the original biblical languages of Hebrew, Aramaic, and Greek. The full Bible has been translated into 717 languages; the New Testament has been translated into an additional 1,582 languages, and Bible portions or stories into 1,196 other languages. Thus at least some portions of the

Bible have been translated into 3,495 languages (*Wikipedia*, n.d., "Bible Translations"; Wycliffe, n.d.). There are mission societies that specialize in capturing languages and dialects in dictionaries. Some of these languages do not even possess an alphabet yet. The Bible Societies have to produce alphabets before they can deliver a portion of the Bible in script for those languages. The Bible Societies are as busy as financially possible to reduce the number of those who do not yet have at least a portion of the Bible in their own language.

There is no longer one single country on earth where the gospel cannot be heard on TV or radio. For that reason, in spite of cruel persecutions the Christian population is quickly growing in North Korea and China, which according to latest findings has sixty million Christians. The Christian Church also grows so quickly in Vietnam, India, and many other countries that the Bible Societies and other Christian publishers find it impossible to provide enough printed teaching material to all who desperately need it.

The Pentecostal movement especially is growing so fast that if its growth continues at the current speed it will match the Roman Catholic Church in membership within ten years. In Canada, the largest but not the only Pentecostal association is the Pentecostal Assemblies of Canada. It is the largest Evangelical group in Canada, with 1,200 churches and a membership total of 250,000 as of May 2022. Germany, Great Britain, and other European countries were once among the most important sources for sending missionaries overseas. Nowadays they have shrunk to become the modern mission fields themselves. However, even in these countries the Pentecostals are the fastest growing Christian association. The reality is that Christianity moves forward victoriously throughout the globe today.

THE SEVENTH SIGN OF THE END TIME AND RETURN OF JESUS CHRIST:
THE GREAT TRIBULATION

FREDERIC THE GREAT once asked his general Joachim Hans von Zieten, a born-again believer in Jesus Christ, "Can you prove to me in one short sentence that there is a God?" Zieten answered him, "Yes, your majesty!" The king encouraged him and replied, "Then say it!" Zieten then said, "The Jews, your majesty!" The king thought about that for a moment, and then said, "Therein he is right!"

If one considers the history of the Jewish people beginning with the Old Testament, as well as in world history, it becomes very hard to deny the existence of God. We have a good example in the Yom Kippur War of 1973 that lasted from October 6 to 25.

On the sixth of October, Israel celebrated the "Day of Atonement." All businesses were closed—even all communication offices, both civil and military. The Syrians and the Egyptians tried to seize the opportunity to destroy Israel quickly. Egypt came with 600,000 soldiers, 2,000 tanks and 550 aircraft across the Suez Canal. Less than five hundred Israeli soldiers with three tanks tried to stop them. At the north the Syrians came with 1,500 tanks. The only defence the Israelis had consisted of 180 aged tanks. This was an impossible situation for Israel, yet within less than a week the Israelis were on their march toward Damascus and they could see the city of Cairo with their binoculars. To this day, many military experts can't understand the miracle of how the Jews accomplished this. There is only one answer: The God of Israel gave them the victory!

Israel will have to go through some more seemingly impossible situations. Among them are the three and a half years of the Great Tribulation, also called "Jacob's Trouble," of which Christ said in Matthew 24:21, *"For then there will be great tribulation, such as has not been since the beginning of the world until this time, no, nor ever shall be."* Israel will cease to exist unless the Lord Jesus Christ comes Himself to give them the victory!

In Zechariah 14:1–5, the last battle is described. The Lord will come at this point, destroy all the enemy nations, and grant Israel the victory.

The Lord Jesus describes the Great Tribulation in Matthew 24:21–22: *"For then there will be great tribulation, such as has not been since the beginning of the world until this time, no, nor ever shall be. And unless those days were shortened [the sum of those days], no flesh would be saved; but for the elect's sake those days will be shortened."*

Antichrist will sign a seven-year treaty with Israel (Daniel 9:27), which will not please God, and He will send punishments as recorded under the seven seals. The seven seals run during the seven years of this treaty, one seal for one year.

First seal and the first year: Antichrist will be victorious in a war and receive dominion.

Second seal and the second year: The Great War continues.

Third seal and the third year: As the product of this war there shall be great inflation.

Fourth seal and the fourth year: As the result of the great inflation, starvation will come. Weakened through this great hunger, an epidemic caused by some wild animals will kill one quarter of the people in Southern Europe, the Middle East, and North Africa.

In the middle of this fourth year, Antichrist will break his treaty with Israel and place an image of himself in the temple of Jerusalem and proclaim that he is God. This will cause a great uproar in Israel. They will rebel against Antichrist, and some Jews will be successful in assassinating him. The Anti-Christian forces will begin a ruthless persecution of the Jews and those Christians who are friends of Israel. God's answer for erecting the statue of Antichrist in the temple, which Jesus calls the *"abomination of desolation"* in Matthew 24:15, is to begin the seven trumpet judgments of Revelation 8:7 to 11:15. These trumpet calls are actually battle signals of the war of God with Antichrist.

The further sequence of the trumpets runs as follows:

1. The first trumpet call: The vegetation is struck with hail, fire, and blood. One third of the trees and all green grass is burned up (Revelation 8:7).

2. The second trumpet call: Something like a burning mountain (a meteor?) falls into the Mediterranean Sea. As a result, one third of the sea looks like blood and one third of the living creatures of the sea die. Also one third of the ships on the sea are destroyed (Revelation 8:8–9).

3. The third trumpet call: A great meteor falls on one third of the rivers and springs, which become bitter. Many people die of these bitter waters (Revelation 8:10–11).

4. The fourth trumpet call: The atmosphere is struck so that one third of the sun, moon, and stars are darkened. An angel flying through the upper atmosphere warns of the next three trumpet calls (Revelation 8:12–13).

5. The fifth trumpet call: Locusts from hell, with tails like scorpions whose stings hurt very much, flood the earth. People are willing to commit suicide because of the pain, but will not succeed. This plague lasts five months. The *"angel of the bottomless pit"* that controls the locusts appears to be Satan himself (Revelation 9:1–12).

6. The sixth trumpet call: The four angels that control the coming of two hundred million soldiers from the east appear to be the heads of four nations that are involved in the Battle of Armageddon. Their armies come from east of the Euphrates River, and they kill about one third of mankind. However, all this suffering does not help to turn peoples' mind toward worshiping God.

They continue with their sins of worshiping demons and idols, with murder, sorcery, theft, and immorality (Revelation 9:13–21).

7. The seventh trumpet call: This is the end of the End Time era. The rapture of the saints Paul refers to as a *"mystery"* in 1 Corinthians 15:50–54 will happen together with the First Resurrection according to 1 Thessalonians 4:14–17. Christ will return with His saints (Revelation 19:11–14), who will declare, *"The kingdoms of this world have become the kingdoms of our Lord and of His Christ, and He shall reign forever and ever!"* (Revelation 11:15).

Through modern medical knowledge, Antichrist will be restored to life. The President of Israel and the High Priest are the Two Witnesses who are called *"the two olive trees"* (Revelation 11:1–14), just as in the Old Testament the governor Zerubbabel and the High Priest Joshua were called (Zechariah 4:11–14). They will lead Israel in its struggle with Antichrist and his forces.

The False Prophet (most likely the Pope of Rome) supports Antichrist and orders all people to wear the number 666 on their right hand or forehead as a token of their faithfulness towards Antichrist (Revelation 13:11–17). Anyone who does not follow orders may not buy or sell, and will be exposed to starvation. Beside the Jews, Christians who support Israel will be persecuted unto death (Revelation 6:9; 13:6–10; 12, 14). God responds by threatening hell for those who accept the number 666 or the name of the Antichrist marked on their bodies (Revelation 14:9–11).

Fifth seal and the fifth year: the persecution of the Jews and Christians who support Israel continues. The martyrs of God ask God to punish Antichrist, the False Prophet, and their crowd (Revelation 6:9–11). God responds by beginning the pouring out of the seven bowls of wrath (Revelation 16:1–21). Many Christian Jews escape from Jerusalem toward the Kingdom of Jordan according to Revelation 12:14–17 and the prophecy of Christ in Matthew 24:16–20.

In Luke 18:7–8, the Lord Jesus says things which apply to the pleas of the martyrs, "…shall God not avenge His own elect who cry out day and night to Him, though He bears long with them? I tell you that He will avenge them speedily."

Sixth seal and the sixth year: Antichrist and the False Prophet are thrown into hell alive (Revelation 19:17–21). Towards the end of this year, the Battle of Armageddon takes place (Revelation 16:12–16). The Russians with their allies will be the victors of this battle. After the battle, they will push towards Jerusalem (Ezekiel chapters thirty-eight and thirty-nine). According to Zechariah 14:2, Jewish resistance will be broken. All will seem lost for the Jews. Daniel 12:7 says of this moment, *"…when the power of the holy people has been completely shattered, all these things shall be finished."*

Suddenly the Lord Jesus Christ will come down from heaven with his followers and turn defeat into an astounding victory. In Isaiah 59:20a it says, *"The Redeemer will come to Zion…,"* while Revelation 16:21 says, *"And great hail from heaven fell upon men, each hailstone about the weight of a talent. Men blasphemed God because of the plague of the hail, since that plague was exceedingly great."* Revelation 14:20 also speaks of this event: *"And the winepress was trampled outside the city [Jerusalem], and blood came out of the winepress, up to the horses' bridles, for one thousand six hundred furlongs"* (184 miles from Jerusalem to the coast of the Mediterranean Sea north of the city). This tremendous red flood will probably come about by blood mixed with the water from the hailstones and red earth.

According to Ezekiel 39:6 and Revelation 19:11–15, Christ will destroy all of rebellious mankind with fire. Malachi 4:1 & 3 says of that moment, *"'For behold, the day is coming, burning like an oven, and all the proud, yes, all who do wickedly will be stubble. And the day which is coming shall burn them up,' says the Lord of Hosts, 'that will leave them neither root nor branch… You shall trample the wicked, for they shall be ashes under the soles of your feet on the day that I do this' says the Lord."*

Seventh seal and the seventh year: silence in heaven for one half hour (Revelation 8:1). Everyone in heaven will quietly watch the coronation of the Lord Jesus Christ as the King of kings and the Lord of lords of the whole world. The Lord Jesus will celebrate the Passover Seder (Matthew 26:29) for the first time after He instituted the communion service drink of the Passover wine. This means that Christ's return will have happened before Easter time.

In Matthew 24:22, Christ says, *"And unless those days were shortened, no flesh would be saved; but for the elect's sake those days will be shortened."* According to our knowledge, the total destruction of life on earth could happen anytime by using nuclear weapons. The combined power of nuclear bombs among nations is enough to destroy life on earth many times over. Christ's return will stop this from happening. In Daniel chapter eight, the angel Gabriel gives Daniel 2,300 evening and morning sacrifices, which result in 1,150 days for the run of the Great Tribulation. This means a shortening from the calendar time of 1,260 days (Daniel 12:7—three and a half years) by 110 days. It is because of this shortening of days that Christ's return is placed within the sixth seal instead of the seventh seal, while His return happens under the seventh trumpet in Revelation 11:15 and at the end of the seven bowls of wrath in Revelation 19:11–16.

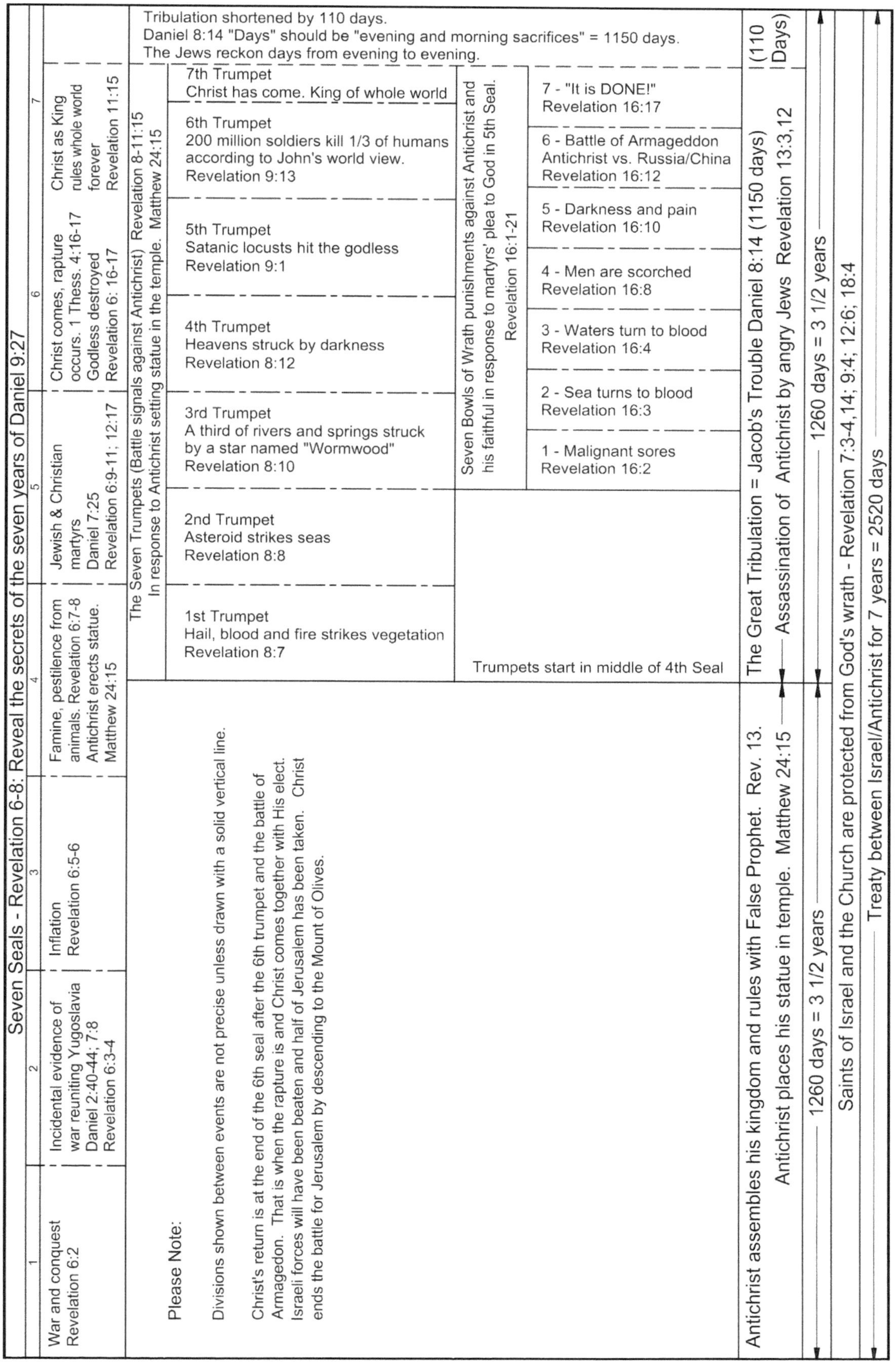

Seven Seals - Revelation 6-8: Reveal the secrets of the seven years of Daniel 9:27

1	2	3	4	5	6	7
War and conquest Revelation 6:2	Incidental evidence of war reuniting Yugoslavia Daniel 2:40-44; 7:8 Revelation 6:3-4	Inflation Revelation 6:5-6	Famine, pestilence from animals. Revelation 6:7-8 Antichrist erects statue. Matthew 24:15	Jewish & Christian martyrs Daniel 7:25 Revelation 6:9-11; 12:17	Christ comes, rapture occurs. 1 Thess. 4:16-17 Godless destroyed Revelation 6: 16-17	Christ as King rules whole world forever Revelation 11:15

Tribulation shortened by 110 days.
Daniel 8:14 "Days" should be "evening and morning sacrifices" = 1150 days.
The Jews reckon days from evening to evening.

The Seven Trumpets (Battle signals against Antichrist) Revelation 8-11:15
In response to Antichrist setting statue in the temple. Matthew 24:15

- 1st Trumpet — Hail, blood and fire strikes vegetation — Revelation 8:7
- 2nd Trumpet — Asteroid strikes seas — Revelation 8:8
- 3rd Trumpet — A third of rivers and springs struck by a star named "Wormwood" — Revelation 8:10
- 4th Trumpet — Heavens struck by darkness — Revelation 8:12
- 5th Trumpet — Satanic locusts hit the godless — Revelation 9:1
- 6th Trumpet — 200 million soldiers kill 1/3 of humans according to John's world view. Revelation 9:13
- 7th Trumpet — Christ has come. King of whole world

Trumpets start in middle of 4th Seal

Seven Bowls of Wrath punishments against Antichrist and his faithful in response to martyrs' plea to God in 5th Seal. Revelation 16:1-21

- 1 - Malignant sores — Revelation 16:2
- 2 - Sea turns to blood — Revelation 16:3
- 3 - Waters turn to blood — Revelation 16:4
- 4 - Men are scorched — Revelation 16:8
- 5 - Darkness and pain — Revelation 16:10
- 6 - Battle of Armageddon Antichrist vs. Russia/China — Revelation 16:12
- 7 - "It is DONE!" — Revelation 16:17

Please Note:

Divisions shown between events are not precise unless drawn with a solid vertical line.

Christ's return is at the end of the 6th seal after the 6th trumpet and the battle of Armagedon. That is when the rapture is and Christ comes together with His elect. Israeli forces will have been beaten and half of Jerusalem has been taken. Christ ends the battle for Jerusalem by descending to the Mount of Olives.

Antichrist assembles his kingdom and rules with False Prophet. Rev. 13.
Antichrist places his statue in temple. Matthew 24:15
— 1260 days = 3 1/2 years —

The Great Tribulation = Jacob's Trouble Daniel 8:14 (1150 days)
Assassination of Antichrist by angry Jews Revelation 13:3,12
— 1260 days = 3 1/2 years —

(110 Days)

Saints of Israel and the Church are protected from God's wrath - Revelation 7:3-4,14; 9:4; 12:6; 18:4
Treaty between Israel/Antichrist for 7 years = 2520 days

Figure 15: Chronological Chart of Events in Revelation

NOTES

THE EIGHTH SIGN OF THE END TIME AND RETURN OF JESUS CHRIST:
THE RETURN OF JESUS CHRIST

IN THIS CHAPTER we are concentrating on biblical sources about the return of the Lord Jesus Christ, though in past chapters we have already examined a fair number of Scriptural sources on this topic. According to Revelation 6:11, the Lord Jesus Christ will not come before the last Christian has suffered the martyr's death, and the last Jew has come to Israel according to Ezekiel 39:28. In light of this information, how can so many pastors claim that the Lord Jesus Christ can come at any moment now, since all the prophecies until His return are supposed to be fulfilled? They are either ignorant of biblical prophecy or outright dishonest in what they say.

There is one other item that limits the time of Christ's return: the temple in Jerusalem is not restored yet, and since the Lord says through the prophet Malachi in chapter 3, verse 1b, *"…And the Lord, whom you seek, will suddenly come to His temple…,"* it is not possible that Christ will return to earth before that temple has been rebuilt. The second coming of the Lord Jesus Christ occurs with the end of the Roman Catholic Church, the demise of Antichrist and his False Prophet, and the end of the Great Tribulation.

In 2 Peter 3:1–11, Peter says in regard to the seeming delay of our Lord's return,

> *Beloved, I now write to you this second epistle (in both of which I stir up your pure minds by way of reminder), that you may be mindful of the words which were spoken before by the holy prophets, and of the commandment of us, the apostles of the Lord and Savior, knowing this first: that scoffers will come in the last days, walking according to their own lusts, and saying, "Where is the promise of His coming? For since the fathers fell asleep, all things continue as they were from the beginning of creation." For this they willfully forget: that by the word of God the heavens were of old, and the earth standing out of water and in the water, by which the world that then existed perished, being flooded with water. But the heavens and the earth which are now preserved by the same word, are reserved for fire until the day of judgment and perdition of ungodly men.*
>
> *But, beloved, do not forget this one thing, that with the Lord one day is as a thousand years, and a thousand years as one day. The Lord is not slack*

> *concerning His promise, as some count slackness, but is longsuffering toward us, not willing that any should perish but that all should come to repentance.*
>
> *But the day of the Lord will come as a thief in the night, in which the heavens will pass away with great noise, and the elements will melt with fervent heat; both the earth and the works that are in it will be burned up. Therefore, since all these things will be dissolved, what manner of persons ought you to be in holy conduct and godliness.*

According to Zechariah chapter fourteen, the Lord will return when the military of Israel is completely and hopelessly beaten, when half of Jerusalem is in the enemy's hands (v. 2). At that point, the Lord Jesus will come down from heaven with the heavenly host (Revelation chapter 19, verses 11–16). Zechariah 12:2–4, 9 says the following:

> *"Behold, I will make Jerusalem a cup of drunkenness to all the surrounding peoples, when they lay siege against Judah and Jerusalem. And it shall happen in that day that I will make Jerusalem a very heavy stone for all peoples; all who would heave it away will surely be cut to pieces, though all nations of the earth are gathered against it. In that day," says the Lord, "I will strike every horse with confusion, and its rider with madness; I will open My eyes on the house of Judah, and will strike every horse of the peoples with blindness… It shall be in that day that I will seek to destroy all the nations that come against Jerusalem."*

At this point in time, the seventh trumpet will sound. The dead in Christ will rise first, to be followed in seconds by the living Christians who will be raptured (1 Thessalonians 4:15–17) and changed into celestial bodies (1 Corinthians 15:51–52) to meet the Lord in the air, which *must* happen at this time or else even the Christians would perish, for the Lord Jesus will destroy the rebellious unbelievers by fire (Ezekiel 39:6; Malachi 4:1–3).

Please note: According to Dr. Alexander Reese (1957), it has been the general teaching of the Church for 1,800 years that the rapture will happen at the time mentioned above. John Darby of the Plymouth Brethren published about the Pre-Tribulation Rapture teaching in the September 1830 issue of *The Morning Watch*. The early disciples of this teaching called it a *"new doctrine,"* and it was gobbled up by a lot of Evangelicals hook, line, and sinker, instead of realizing that all doctrines of the New Testament were already known, and that any "new doctrine" must be looked at with suspicion and labelled false. C. H. Spurgeon once said: "There is nothing new in theology except what is false." Dr. James McKeever (1987) quotes veteran missionary H.A. Baker, John Wesley White, Corrie Ten Boom, Demos Shakarian and Richard Wurmbrand, who all say that this new teaching has caused a lot of suffering and even death among Chinese and Hungarian Christians who did not run to escape, hoping that the Pre-Tribulation Rapture would remove them from the advancing Communists. The Roman Catholic Church, Anglican Church, and Lutheran Church all still teach the Post-Tribulation Rapture.

If God raptures the last generation of Christians to escape persecution, He would have to apologize to the many millions of Christian martyrs of twenty centuries for not rapturing them out of harm's way. Therefore, it is not likely that there will be a pre-tribulation rapture. In fact, the following verses of Revelation prove that Christians will not be raptured before the Great Tribulation; however, they will be protected from God's wrath according to Revelation 7:3–17; 9:4; 12:14; 18:4.

In Revelation 6:9, the story of the Fifth Seal, which happens in the fifth year of the treaty between Israel and Antichrist, it is said: *"When He opened the fifth seal, I saw under the altar the souls* [actually, the spirits] *of those who had been slain for the word of God and for the testimony which they held,"* and in Revelation 7:14, we learn that *"These are the ones who come out of the great tribulation, and washed their robes and made them white in the blood of the Lamb"*—that is, of Christ—so these people were Christian martyrs. There is no report in Revelation of any conversions to Christ happening during the Great Tribulation. Thus, it must be assumed that these martyrs were Christians before entering the Great Tribulation. This indicates that there were Christians within the Great Tribulation. This argument is supported by Revelation 7:3–4 & 14; 9:4; 12:6; and 18:4. Revelation 7:9–17 makes it incidentally clear that this "multitude" of martyrs represents the Church during the Great Tribulation.

The fifth book of the famous Matthew Henry Commentary, written in 1721, says this of Mark 13:24 on page 543: "after that tribulation," and about the rapture of the Church in verse 27: "The gathering together of all elect to him [Christ]; He shall send his angels, and gather together his elect to him to meet him in the air, 1. Thessalonians 4:17. They shall be fetched from one end of the world to the other, so none shall be missing from that general assembly."

In the same book it refers to Luke 17: 34 on page 771: "…two in one bed, one taken and the other left, one snatched out of the burning and taken into a place of safety, while the other is left to perish in the common ruin."

I have read the same verses in the German, Swedish, Norwegian, Danish, Dutch and Low German Bibles of today. I can understand all these languages and they agree with Matthew Henry's take 100%.

Back to Christ's return. The unbelievers' bodies will become ashes under Israel's feet according to Malachi 4:3. Perhaps children up to twelve or thirteen years of age will be saved because they are under the age of accountability. Probably they will also be raptured. However, the Bible is silent about this issue. All we know is that our Lord Jesus said in Luke 18:16, *"Let the little children come to Me, and do not forbid them; for of such is the kingdom of God."* So they will be saved at His coming too.

Then the people of Israel will open their eyes and recognize that the Lord Jesus is indeed their true Messiah. This is written about in Zechariah 12:10–13:1:

> *And I will pour on the house of David and on the inhabitants of Jerusalem the Spirit of grace and supplication; then they will look on Me whom they pierced. Yes, they will mourn for Him as one mourns for his only son, and grieve for Him as one grieves for a firstborn. In that day there shall be a great mourning in Jerusalem, like the mourning at Hadad Rimmon in the plain of Megiddo. And the land shall mourn, every family by itself: the family of the house of David by itself, and their wives by themselves; the family of the house of Nathan by itself, and their wives by themselves; the family of the house of Levi by itself, and their wives by themselves; the family of Shimei by itself, and their wives by themselves; all the families that remain, every family by itself, and their wives by themselves.*
>
> *In that day a fountain shall be opened for the house of David and for the inhabitants of Jerusalem, for sin and for uncleanness.*

In Zechariah 13:6 it is written, *"And one will say to him: 'What are these wounds between your arms?' Then he will answer: 'Those with which I was wounded in the house of my friends.'"* This is the repentance of Israel for what they have done to Jesus Christ in unbelief. By this time, the Lord Jesus has arrived on earth on the Mount of Olives (Zechariah 14:4). The mountain has been split from east to west, making a very large valley into which the remaining Jews of Jerusalem have fled. In the next chapter, we will learn what happens after this.

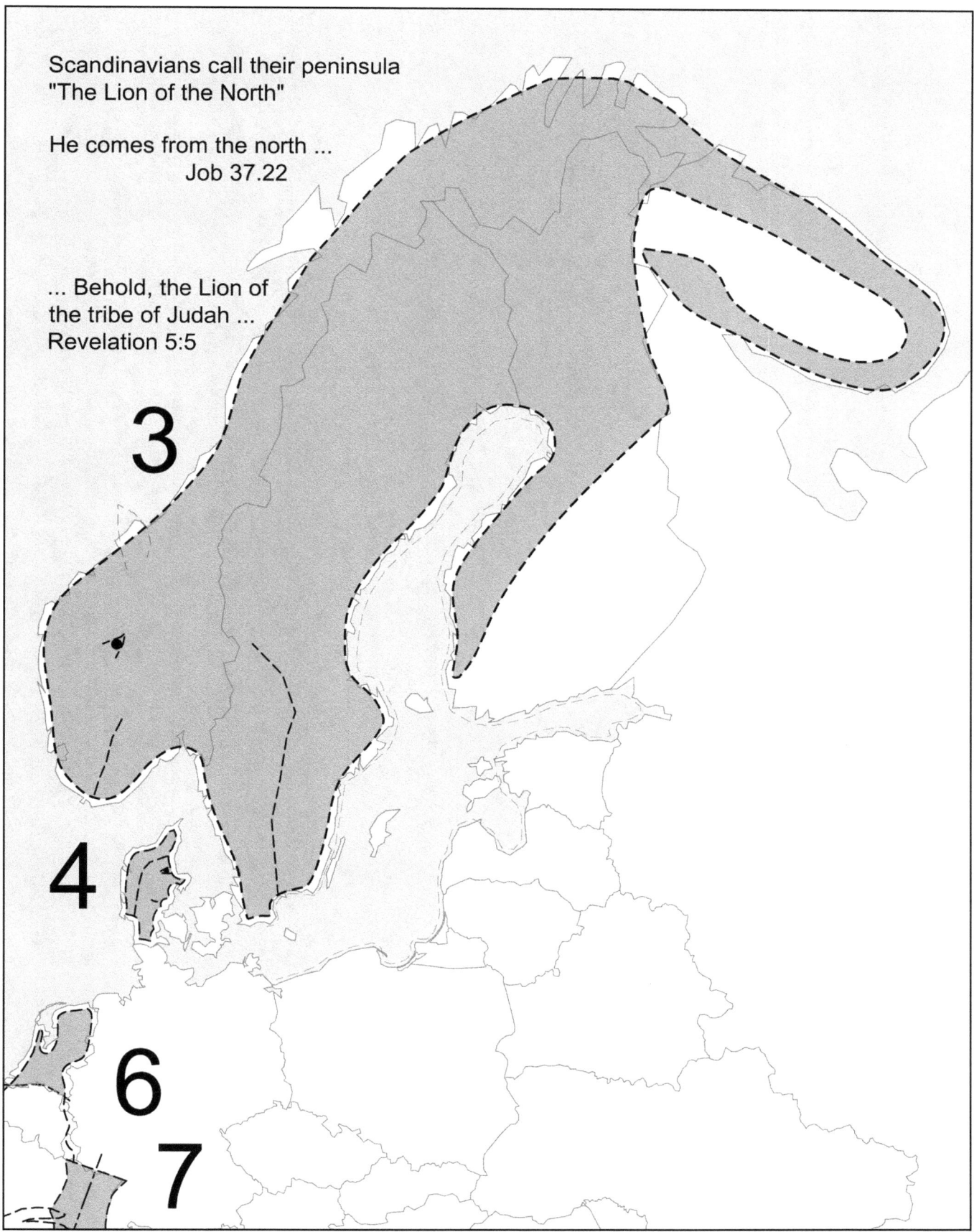

Figure 16: Scandinavia – The "Lion of Judah"

NOTES

END TIME TO HEAVEN:
WHAT HAPPENS IMMEDIATELY AFTER CHRIST'S RETURN

WHILE IT IS true that today we cannot know the exact time of Christ's return, the people living on the day when Israel confronts Antichrist (Daniel 9:27) over setting up his image will know the exact time of Christ's return based on numbers given in the book of Daniel chapters eight, nine, and twelve, plus the information given in the book of Revelation chapters eleven, twelve, and thirteen. The reason for this is probably so that those suffering in the Great Tribulation can know when their torment will end.

However, this same time information can help us fit together the run of the treaty between Antichrist and Israel in years, months, and days, to get some idea of how things fit together. I begin with the highest number, the 1335 days of the end of the Great Tribulation, and work my way backward from this end number to the beginning. So here it goes:

The 1335 days in Daniel 12:12 are counted from the day on which Antichrist sets up his image three and a half years after the signing of the treaty between Israel and himself. On the 1335th day, the Lord Jesus will be crowned King of kings of the whole world. On that day, He will also celebrate the Passover Seder for the first time again after his departure for heaven, as He tells His disciples in Matthew 26:29: *"But I say to you, I will not drink of this fruit of the vine from now on until that day when I drink it new with you in My Father's kingdom."* Passover is usually celebrated in April. So the Lord Jesus has come, and He can celebrate the Passover Seder now with His disciples as He has promised. If Passover falls on April 15th for example, we count 45 days back (the difference between 1335 and 1290 days) and come to the end of February, which is the 1290th day, the day the temple is finished being cleansed of the *"abomination of desolation."* Then we trace back 110 days according to Daniel 8:14 note 1 *("two thousand three hundred evening-mornings")*, plus thirty days, the difference between 1290 and 1260, for a total of 140 days and we arrive at the coming of Christ, which could happen at about the 10th of October. The numbers given above indicate also that the second three and a half years, the Great Tribulation, begins around the middle of July, and the first three and a half years of the treaty between Antichrist and Israel begin in January, though *in which year we do not know.* However, this gives us an idea how the seven-year contract of Antichrist with Israel and the return of Christ will run.

Now I will present the events of this time from beginning to end.

January: The seven-year treaty of Antichrist with Israel is signed (Daniel 9:27). 1260 days later (three and a half years) in **July,** Antichrist sets up his image in the temple and the Jews rebel. Antichrist starts the persecution of Jews and Christians who are friendly to Israel. God replies with the beginning of the trumpet battle calls. The Great Tribulation begins. 1150 days later, Jesus Christ comes, shortening the sufferings of Israel and Christians of the 1260 days by 110 days. Because of this shortening, Christ returns in **October** under the sixth seal. Finally, the Jews recognize Jesus as their Messiah (Zechariah 12:10 & 13:6), and at the end of **February,** the temple cleansing ends at the 1290th day after the temple desecration. Forty-five days later, the 1335th day after Antichrist's temple desecration, **April 15th**, seven months after His return, the crowning of Christ as the King of kings of the whole world and the Passover service with Christ's disciples will take place, in a year we do not know.

On the same October day that Christ returns, the seventh angel will pour out his seventh bowl of wrath into the air and a loud voice will come out of heaven from the throne, saying, *"It Is Done!"* The Great Tribulation will be finished. *"And there were noises and thunderings and lightnings; and there was a great earthquake, such a mighty and great earthquake as had not occurred since men were on the earth"* (Revelation 16:17–18).

And to the vultures God will say,

> *Assemble yourselves and come; gather together from all sides to My sacrificial meal which I am sacrificing for you, a great sacrificial meal on the mountains of Israel, that you may eat flesh and drink blood. You shall eat the flesh of the mighty, drink the blood of the princes of the earth, of rams and lambs, of goats and bulls, all of them fatlings of Bashan. You shall eat fat till you are full, and drink blood till you are drunk, at My sacrificial meal which I am sacrificing for you. You shall be filled at My table with horses and riders, with mighty men and with all the men of war.* (Ezekiel 39:17–20; see also Revelation 19:17)

This powerful earthquake will reshape the topography of the Holy Land according to Zechariah 14:10: *"All the land shall be turned into a plain from Geba to Rimnon south of Jerusalem." "Every valley shall be exalted and every mountain and hill brought low…"* (Isaiah 40:4). *"Jerusalem shall be raised up…"* (Zechariah 14:10). *"In the visions of God He took me into the land of Israel and set me on a very high mountain; on it toward the south was something like the structure of a city"* (Ezekiel 40:2). This city is Jerusalem.

The new temple appears to be mounted on top of this high mountain (described from Ezekiel 40:5 all the way to chapter 47). This temple appears suddenly. It looks as if God Himself built it and set it on the mountain according to Christ's statement in John 2:19, which also can be applied here: *"Destroy this temple, and in three days I will raise it up."* It replaces the temple that was desecrated by Antichrist. Finally, the word spoken by the patriarch Jacob in Genesis 28:22 will come to pass: *"…this stone which I have set as a pillar shall be God's house…"*

This place on the mountain on which the new temple will stand is called *"Beth-El"* (Genesis 28:19, *"the House of God"*). The main gate of this temple faces east. From thence a brook of fresh water flows that becomes a river which parts the city of Jerusalem into three, because the river divides itself into two branches. One branch flows to the Mediterranean Sea and the other branch flows down through the new valley that was created by Christ by splitting Mount Olivet in two. It flows down into the Jordan Valley and empties into the Dead Sea. This will "heal" the Dead Sea so that saltwater fish can live in it. The Dead Sea will not contain fresh water, but its salt content will be equal to the Mediterranean Sea, because the same fish species will be found in the Dead Sea. However, the uttermost southern bay will remain very salty. On both banks of the river, fruit trees will grow whose fruit and leaves will serve for food and medicine. All this information comes from Zechariah chapter 14:10 and Ezekiel 47:1–12.

END TIME TO HEAVEN II:
THE MILLENNIUM

BEFORE THE THOUSAND years of Christ's rule over the entire world, Antichrist and his false prophet will be cast alive into the lake of fire (Revelation 19:20). An angel will come down from heaven and bind Satan with a great chain for a thousand years. The kingdom of Christ that lasts for one thousand years is also known as the Millennium. It begins with the crowning of the Lord Jesus Christ as the King of kings and the Lord of lords, the only ruler of the entire world. He will sit on His throne at Jerusalem.

The land of Israel will look different from today. Most of it will be a plain, and the most prominent mountain will rise beginning at the northern part of Jerusalem. The mountain's name will be Beth-El (House of God) after the former town on its top and in memory of the patriarch Jacob's promise made in Genesis 28:19–22. On its top there will be the millennial temple built by God, and according to Ezekiel 43:13–27, animal sacrifices will be made upon its altar. This causes us Christians a theological problem, seeing that according to Hebrews 9:22–28 and 10:1–4, no animal sacrifices can atone for our sins, and Christ is the one and only sacrifice for all our sins. Well, the animal sacrifices during the Millennium are not sin offerings, but offerings of love and thanksgiving—feasts for the people.

The whole earth will be renovated as it was at the creation. Psalm 104:30 says, *"…You renew the face of the earth."* Lifespans shall be expanded according to Isaiah 65:20: *"No more shall an infant from there live but a few days, nor an old man who has not fulfilled his days; for the child shall die one hundred years old, but the sinner being one hundred years old shall be accursed."* The passage continues,

> *They shall build houses and inhabit them; they shall plant vineyards and eat their fruit. They shall not build and another inhabit; they shall not plant and another eat; for as the days of a tree, so shall be the days of My people, and My elect shall long enjoy the work of their hands. They shall not labour in vain, nor bring forth children for trouble; for they shall be the descendants of the blessed of the Lord, and their offspring with them.*
>
> *It shall come to pass that before they call, I will answer; and while they are still speaking, I will hear.* (v. 21–24)

Even among the animals there will be changes: *"The wolf and the lamb shall feed together, the lion shall eat straw like the ox, and dust shall be the serpent's food"* (v. 25).

Now there will be nations full of children up to age thirteen with few adults, since all the rebellious adults will have been destroyed. Only adults whom God knows would have been open to accepting Christ, if they had had the chance to do so, will survive to enter the Millennium. In Micah 4:1–2 it says,

> *Now it shall come to pass in the latter days that the mountain of the Lord's house shall be established on top of the mountains, and shall be exalted above the hills; and peoples shall flow to it. Many nations shall come and say, "Come, and let us go up to the mountain of the Lord, to the house of the God of Jacob; He will teach us His ways, and we shall walk in His paths."*

"…in those days ten men from every language of the nations shall grasp the sleeve of a Jewish man, saying, 'Let us go with you, for we have heard that God is with you'" (Zechariah 8:23). They will be cared for by the Israeli military according to Micah 5:7–8: *"Then the remnant of Jacob shall be in the midst of many peoples, like dew from the Lord, like showers on the grass, that tarry for no man, nor wait for the sons of man. And the remnant of Jacob shall be among the Gentiles, in the midst of many peoples, like a lion among the beasts of the forest."* Isaiah 66:19 says, *"I will set a sign among them [the nations]; and those among them who escape [the Israelis] I will send to the nations: to Tarshish and Pul and Lud, who draw the bow [the Israeli military], and Tubal and Javan, to the coastlands afar off who have not heard My fame nor seen My glory."* They will probably be supported by angels, for the task before them is overwhelming.

Only a third of the people of Israel will survive into the Millennium according to Zechariah 13:9: *"I will bring the one third through the fire, will refine them as silver is refined, and test them as gold is tested. They will call on My name, and I will answer them. I will say, 'This is my people'; and each one will say, 'The Lord is my God.'"*

Israel will for the first time in its long history possess the entirety of the land promised by God in Genesis 15:18 and Exodus 23:31: from the Red Sea to the River of Egypt (meaning the Brook of Egypt—this is the Wadi Al-Arish), the Sea of the Philistines (meaning the Mediterranean Sea), and from the desert on the east of the Jordan Valley to the River (the Euphrates). This means that some of Jordan and most of Syria will become Israeli territory. According to Ezekiel chapter 48, the land will be divided up from the North, to the tribe of Dan, then the tribe of Asher, followed by the tribe of Manasseh, followed by the tribe of Ephraim, followed by the tribe of Reuben, followed by the tribe of Judah. This will be followed by the Holy District being populated by the priests, the Levites, with Jerusalem in the centre of this district, and the "prince's" portion next, followed by the tribes of Benjamin, Simeon, Issachar, Zebulun, and Gad.

The "Prince" in Ezekiel 46:16-17 cannot be Jesus Christ, but His earthly representative to Israel, for he has sons. It does not make sense to spiritualize this problem and say the "sons" are some elect Christians, for we are not Christ's sons but His brothers according to Luke 8:21 and Romans 8:29. He must also be a descendant of the family of David to qualify for this position. What we have here is a phenomenon that appears often in Scripture, in that there are two persons for one ministry: Abraham and Melchizedek, Moses and Aaron, Samuel and David, Elijah and Elisha, Ezra and Nehemiah, Joshua and Zerubbabel, John the Baptist and Jesus Christ, the Prince and the King of kings—Jesus Christ—and the Two Witnesses of Revelation chapter eleven who are the "Governor" (the President or Prime Minister of Israel) and the High Priest, according to Zechariah 4:11–14. These last two are mentioned in Revelation 11:4, which is identical with Zechariah 4:2–4 and 11–14. It is a rule of Bible interpretation to compare text with text of the same context (Rule 13), which I have done here.

THE MILLENNNIUM

The martyrs of the Great Tribulation, according to Revelation 20:4, will rule with Christ for one thousand years. When the Millennium comes to its end, God will test whether the people who have enjoyed life on this renewed earth under the sovereignty of Christ will remain faithful to Christ or not. For this purpose, Satan will be let loose to tempt them according to Revelation 20:7–10. He will have great results, especially in Gog and Magog, which are usually identified with Russia. They will surround the saints and Jerusalem. God will react again with fire and consume the enemies (Revelation 20:7–9). Then Satan will be cast into the lake of fire and brimstone, and together with Antichrist and the False Prophet they will be tormented day and night forever (v. 10).

Please note: Satan, Antichrist and the False Prophet will be tormented forever. Some people deny that there will be any eternal existence, claiming that all life will be exterminated at death. Well, the text here claims the opposite—why? The reason why torment will be felt forever is that the spirits of people and angels exist forever. The spirit in a person is the actual life in a human or spiritual body. Paul calls the body a *"tent"* in 2 Corinthians 5:1, and Peter does the same in 2 Peter 1:13. So the real "you" is not the body you wear, but the spirit that lives in your body. It is the spirit in you that makes the eyes see, the ears hear—in short, gives sense to all your five senses. It is the spirit in you that makes the brain think.

Remove the spirit from the body and the body is dead! While the human body perishes, the spirit never does because the spirit is eternal, just as it says in Ecclesiastes 12:7: *"Then the dust [your body] will return to the earth as it was, and the spirit will return to God who gave it."* It will remain there forever! Because spirits do not die, they can be tormented eternally!

NOTES

END TIME TO HEAVEN III:
THE GREAT WHITE THRONE JUDGMENT

THE JUDGMENT AT the Great White Throne will decide the future of every individual ever born. According to Evangelical belief, only people who have accepted the Lord Jesus Christ will go to heaven. All others will go to hell.

This is a very flippant attitude that does not take in account the conditions and possibilities of billions of people who never had the chance to hear the gospel and decide for or against Christ, whether before Christ's time or after, even up to our time. It would be cruel of God to condemn all these people indiscriminately to hell. No, my God is good and just, and He will review every person's life to decide where they will spend eternity.

First, let's look at the guarantee that will help a person to end up in heaven. The Lord Jesus speaks about it in Matthew 25:31–46 in the story about the sheep and the goats. Both types did the same things (compare verses 35–36 and 44), but the goats were rejected. Why? Because the "sheep," representing God's children, have a "knowing" recognition and relationship with Him, while the "goats" do not have this relationship with Him and so do not "know" God, and God therefore does not "know" them. So we learn that it is not deeds that lead to a heavenly reward, but a relationship with God.

This complies with the two main commandments of the Bible: *"You shall love the Lord your God with all your heart, with all your soul, and with all your might"* (Deuteronomy 6:5) and *"…you shall love your neighbor as yourself"* (Leviticus 19:18). The Lord Jesus confirmed these two commandments for the New Testament in Matthew 22:37–40. In Micah 6:8, God speaks: *"He has shown you, O man, what is good; and what does the Lord require of you but to do justly, to love mercy, and to walk humbly with your God?"*

Atheists make fun of the idea that God will judge every person, because it would take very many years to judge all the many billions of people! But they are wrong. Based on the principles above, it will pass very quickly. At the Great White Throne you will have to answer these two questions: What did you do with Jesus Christ in your life? Did you have a personal relationship with Him, taking Him as your Saviour and Lord and following Him faithfully, or not?

Your answer to this question will determine if you belong to the saved (sheep) or to the lost (goats).

The night of my eleventh birthday, I had a terrible dream about the last judgment that I will never forget. I did not dream this dream because I had been thinking about the last judgment at the Great White Throne during the previous day, for my birthday falls on the twenty-third of December, when a child is thinking about Christmas. So it seems that God gave me this dream.

FROM THE END TIME TO HEAVEN

In the dream, I emerged from a grave dressed in a white garment. Around the cemetery, others arose too, all dressed in white. We walked silently toward a grassy hill where millions of people stood together, and you could hear the murmur of people talking. All looked into the sky. There was a long cloud; a giant hand was seen above it and a giant foot was seen below. Suddenly the cloud parted in the middle to reveal a giant angel standing in midair, and he said with a loud voice: "You are all lost and you will go into damnation!" Then blackness was all around us and we all screamed aloud in fear. I woke up from my own screams, soaking wet from sweat on my whole body. How grateful I was that this was just a dream! It is possible to be religious (the white garment) and still be lost if one lacks a personal relationship with Christ.

It is interesting to note that God does not pay attention to the many individual sins of the lost. He has to do this to be just, for He does not reckon the individual sins of the saved, casting them into the sea of forgetfulness (Micah 7:19). So they are not mentioned anymore. All He asks is a personal relationship with Him. It is the lack of such a relationship with God that sends the lost into hell, not their particular sins.

According to Christ's word in Matthew 25:41, hell is not planned for people but for the devil and his angels. If a person ends up in hell, it is their own fault. According to Luke 4:5–6, the earth was given into Satan's stewardship when he was the archangel Lucifer, so every person living on earth is his subject, unless you have taken the Lord Jesus Christ as your Saviour and Lord. Therefore all the lost people will go where Satan goes—into hell!

However, in contrast to all that has been written so far, the righteous God will scrutinize the billions of people who have not had a chance to hear about Jesus Christ and therefore could not make a decision for Him. He knows which of them would gladly have taken the Lord Jesus Christ as their Saviour and Lord if they would have had a chance. These people will not be sent into hell, but there is also a future for them in eternity as we will see in the next chapter, "Finally in Heaven!"

This news may cause you to wonder: if these people are being saved without having received Christ as their Saviour, why do we send out missionaries, some of whom are dying a martyr's death? The answer is simple.

First, our Lord Jesus has given His life on the cross with the potential of saving all people from going to hell, including the rebellious unbelievers (Matthew 18:11 & John 12:47). To reach them for Christ, many Christians will die as martyrs. Some of these rebels will respond to the Gospel and be saved out of the devil's grasp. This is the reason for Christian missionary work. Those that resist will have no excuse at the White Throne judgment to prevent them from being condemned to hell.

Secondly, our heavenly Father wants to enlarge His family by as many converts as possible, but only those who accept Jesus Christ as their Saviour and Lord will become sons and daughters of the family of God. They will be changed into celestial bodies to be like God. However, as for the unreached people, of whom there are billions, those of them who would have accepted Christ if they would have had the chance will not be lost. They will be resurrected with their physical bodies and form the nations in heaven. In Revelation chapter twenty-two you will find a confirmation of my teaching here, for it clearly says that the leaves of the tree of life are for the healing of the nations. Christians do not need healing, since they will have celestial bodies that will never get sick.

Atheists sneer at the thought of hell. Today, few preachers preach about hell. Some of them have their doubts about it too. Is there really a hell or not?

There are four different words in the Bible for three kinds of hell. The first one is a Hebrew word that means the abode of the dead: *Sheol.* The same meaning in Greek is the word *Hades.* Then there is the Greek word *Tartarus,* which is held to be the prison for the fallen angels. Finally there is the Hebrew word *Gehenna,* which means the eternal hell for the devil and all the lost people.

THE GREAT WHITE THRONE JUDGMENT

Is There Really a Hell?

There are human experiences that clearly demonstrate that there is a hell. A famous case happened under the ministry of the well-known Evangelical Lutheran pastor Johann Christoph Blumhardt the Elder (1805–1880). He and his household prayed for a woman of his congregation who was not saved and had passed away through suicide. He said, "I will not leave this person in hell." So they prayed for her for eight hours. Then the woman breathed and moaned: "Please keep on praying and do not leave me in this fire!" They kept on praying until she was pulled out of the fire of hell. She confessed that she was in hell because of unforgiveness in her heart, greed, and the lack of a personal relationship with Christ. She accepted the Lord Jesus Christ as her Saviour and Lord.

Another case is that of Dr. Maurice Rawlings (easily found through a Google search), a heart specialist and atheist who educated other physicians. He had a lot of experiences with dying patients, some of whom had good experiences of the beyond, while others had bad ones. It was the terrifying experiences of the bad cases where people claimed to be in the fire of hell that led him to believe in God, heaven, and hell, and write a book about his experiences.

Then there is Bill Wiese. He claims that he went to hell in 1998 at 3 A.M. and remained there for twenty-three minutes. He has seen the fires and the sufferers, and experienced a part of the tortures that happen in hell.

Where is hell? The Bible hints that hell is deep down in the earth in Deuteronomy 32:22, where hell is situated in the lowest place (considered from the surface of earth). This agrees completely with the findings of science, which tells us that there is a mighty hot fire in the centre of the earth.

What is going to happen to hell after the Judgment of the Great White Throne? The old earth, which has hell at its centre, will be shot out of the universe and into the black empty cosmos according to Revelation 20:11. What a horrendous fate for all those in hell to float eternally in the black cosmos! That is why everyone who reads this and has not yet taken the Lord Jesus Christ as your Saviour and Lord should do so quickly, lest you miss the opportunity to get your name written in the Book of Life (Revelation 20:12)!

Now we come to the question: **"Is there really a heaven?"** According to the last two chapters of Revelation, there is a heaven, and it has a lot of things that resemble a planet: water, rocks, jewels, and time concepts like twelve months, which contain of course weeks, days, hours, minutes, and seconds. In heaven many things live: plants, animals and people, angels, and God Himself. So heaven must also have an atmosphere that is beneficial to living beings.

Does somebody know where the planet Heaven is located? In Isaiah 14:13, God says that His throne is upon the mountain of the congregation in the farthest north. So in heaven there are also mountains, and the planet is located in the farthest north of the universe (meaning the direction of a straight line that goes into outer space directly above the North Pole). In the oldest book of the Bible, the book of Job (about 1600 B. C.), Job says that there is an empty place in the far north of the universe (26:7). How could Job know this? Clearly only by inspiration, for in his time there existed no telescope to let him see it.

Dr. Hank Lindstrom of Bibleline Ministries writes,

> Here is another amazing scientific fact. There is an empty place or void in the north of our universe. It was first discovered with the 200 inch telescope on Mount Palomar, California, and is now being studied by three separate observatories across the country (USA). This empty place has been found to be so large that it could contain 2,000 milky ways. The Milky Way is 100,000 light years across.

That would mean that light traveling at 186,000 miles per second takes 100,000 years to travel from one end of the Milky Way to the other. We believe that heaven is located in that void in the north of our universe. (Lindstrom, n.d.)

END TIME TO HEAVEN IV:
FINALLY IN HEAVEN!

MOST OF OUR information about heaven is found in Revelation chapters twenty-one and twenty-two. In heaven there will be things that previously existed in the Millennium. It is typical for things in God's word to come in groups of two, as mentioned before regarding people in ministry and other subjects in the Bible. According to Revelation 21:2, the New Jerusalem will be transferred to the New Earth, so the new heaven will exist on the new earth. As mentioned in the previous chapter, in this New Heaven there will be a new nature with plants, animal life, as well as people and angels. What is gloriously new is that God the Father will no longer be invisible, but will be seen.

There will be an intimate relationship between God the Father and His people, to the point that He will even wipe the tears from their eyes according to Revelation 21:4. The same verse emphasizes that there will be no more sorrow, crying, pain, or death. In heaven, the water of life will flow beside the tree of life (21:4; 22:2).

Then the text concentrates on the capital city of heaven, called the "New Jerusalem" and elsewhere the "City of Truth" (Zechariah 8:3). There will not be a temple in that city, according to Revelation 21:22. That does not mean that there will no longer be a temple anywhere, for in Revelation there are several verses speaking of God's temple. Those who come out of the Great Tribulation will serve God in His temple (Revelation 7:15). In this temple there will also be an ark of God's covenant (Revelation 11:19).

Let us continue discussing the city. Its shape will include the same measure for its length, breadth, and height. Most Bible scholars believe that this city represents a cube, which is a mistake. In all places where the Bible talks about a future Jerusalem, it is associated with or likened to a mountain, such as in the previous heaven where the city was called the "Mountain of the Congregation" (Isaiah 14:13). The New Jerusalem will look like a mountain too, being a pyramid—an artificial mountain—with sloping sides where the length, breadth, and height are the same.

The city will have a high wall with three gates on all four sides that are each made of a giant pearl. These gates are named after the twelve tribes of Israel. The city also has twelve foundations named after the twelve apostles of Christ. The foundations consist of various jewels. Its streets are paved with pure gold, and the main street is divided by the River of Life. On both sides of this river grow the trees of life. This river falls in cascades down one side of the pyramid. That must be a very beautiful sight. Its water originates from the throne of God, which sits on the top of the pyramid. What once was written about the city and the river of the Millennium is repeated here in a more glorious way, confirming the biblical principle of twos.

There will be day and night in Heaven—in Revelation 22:2, the word "month" indicates a "moon." Remember that Israel follows a lunar calendar based on the cycles of the moon, and the moon shines generally at night. The text of this verse also indicates a year of twelve months. Transferring this to Revelation 22:2, it appears that the planet Heaven's year is also lunar. Chapter 22:5 indicates that the New Jerusalem needs no night and no sunlight, because God's light illuminates the city twenty-four hours a day.

What will the landscape of heaven look like? Adventists believe that heaven will be a flat plain without any hills or mountains. Revelation 21:1 states that there will be no more sea (oceans). However, there is the River of Life (Revelation 22:1). It comes from the mountaintop of the New Jerusalem. Most likely it flows into a lake. Since one river is mentioned here, it stands to reason that there must be more rivers on Heaven, and they too flow into lakes. How can I state this? Because there are nations on the Planet Heaven consisting of physical people, and they will need a lot of water to sustain life (Revelation 21:24). According to our experiences, many rivers come from glaciers, and these sit on high mountains. So the landscape of Heaven is similar to the beautiful landscapes on earth, except that there will be no more oceans and most likely no more deserts. That is why you can call the landscape on Heaven "The Paradise of God" (Revelation 2:7).

The nations of heaven also live in cities, with the New Jerusalem being the capital of Heaven. On the twenty-eighth of June, 1998, I was transported to heaven for a few minutes. There I saw one of those cities in the distance that was not the New Jerusalem. So, who are the people of the heavenly nations that need the leaves of the Trees of Life in Heaven for their health (Revelation 22:2)? By the Scriptures, we are led to believe that the saints of the Old as well as the New Testament will live in the New Jerusalem.

Who, then, are the people of the other nations on the Planet Heaven? They are the people I mentioned in the last chapter: people who never had a chance to hear about the gospel of our Lord Jesus Christ, because they lived in different ages than Christ on earth, or in different locations. They would have accepted the Lord Jesus Christ as their Saviour and Lord had they been given the chance to do so, and God knows them. Therefore, God will save them and grant them life on the Planet Heaven, also called the "New Earth" (Revelation 21:1). However, they will come to heaven in their physical bodies, not changed into celestial bodies like we Christians will be, as is stated in the Apostolic Creed: "I believe in the resurrection of the flesh." That is why they need the leaves of the Tree of Life for their healing according to Revelation 22:2. These people originate from the 7,378 tribes of earth, so there will be 7,378 new nations on Heaven. Their kings and leaders will be Christians, for Revelation 1:6 tells us that Christians (at least some of us, since it is unclear if this verse applies to all Christians) will be kings and priests in Heaven. See also 1 Peter 2:5.

What kind of "glory and honour" will the kings of the heavenly nations bring to the capital city of Heaven (Revelation 21:26)? I do not think their tribute will be gold, precious stones, et cetera, because eventually the city would be filled up with this stuff. I think it will be fruits and worship, because all the things written about in this chapter are going to last eternally. Just think: you personally, dear reader, will have the chance to be there, provided you accept the Lord Jesus Christ as your personal Saviour and Lord and follow the teachings of the New Testament.

While this is all extremely beautiful and wonderful, the greatest thing is that in Heaven we will finally see the wonderfully beautiful person of God our Father and the Lord Jesus Christ, and He will live among us. He will wipe away all our tears. *"...there shall be no more death, nor sorrow, nor crying. There shall be no more pain, for the former things have passed away"* (Revelation 21:4).

Please note: Contrary to the belief of many Christians, there will still be time in heaven. There is a *day* and a *night* in heaven just like here on earth, because the New Heaven exists on the New Planet Earth. If there will be day and night in eternity, there will also be hours, minutes, and seconds, as well as weeks, months, and years: *"In the middle of its street, and on either side of the river, was the tree of life, which bore twelve fruits, each tree <u>yielding its fruit every month</u>"* (Revelation 22:2, emphasis added). So the song "When the trumpet of the Lord shall sound and time shall be no more…" is misleading. James M. Black, the poet that wrote these words, should have realized that movement requires time. If there is no time, then *all movement ceases*. Trees require time to grow and develop their fruit, which in turn carries seed for the next generation of trees. The water of the River of Life (chapter 22:1) requires time to flow. And Revelation 21:24 says, *"…the nations of those who are saved shall <u>walk</u> in its light, and the kings of the earth <u>bring</u> their glory and honor into it"* (emphasis added). The verb "walk" requires time. So does the verb "bring." Because Revelation 22:2 says *"twelve fruits, each tree yielding its fruit every month,"* it appears that the Planet Heaven has a twelve-month year. Since the word "month" is related to "moon," it appears that Heaven will also have a moon. Taking all the data of this chapter in consideration, it appears that "Eternity" consists of a *non-ending stretch of days*.

The description of this blessed eternity closes with the invitation:

> *He who is unjust, let him be unjust still; he who is filthy, let him be filthy still; he who is righteous, let him be righteous still; he who is holy, let him be holy still…*
> *And the Spirit and the bride say, "Come!" And let him who hears say, "Come!" And let him who thirsts come. Whoever desires, let him take the water of life freely.* (Revelation 22:11, 17)

Amen. Even so, come, Lord Jesus!

NOTES

APPENDIX
OTHER IMPORTANT TOPICS

NOTES

THE CORRECT DATES OF JESUS CHRIST'S LIFE AND PENTECOST
(Written in 2017)

CONCERNING MY METHOD of Scripture interpretation (True Bible, True Science, True History, and Common Sense), I am grateful to the Holy Spirit for His support. I would not like to write something that would be displeasing to Him. I often receive His leading, as represented in this essay.

For thirty years I have tried to find the time of Christ's birth in the times given us by the Prophet Daniel (9:24–27), because I was sure that the dates were hidden somehow within the numbers in that text. However, I did not succeed. I read books that tried to establish the time of Christ's birth, but I did not find their arguments satisfactory.

One day the Holy Spirit spoke to me unexpectedly. At that moment I was not thinking about this problem, but the Holy Spirit just spoke out of the blue:

> Werner, if you want to find the year of the birthday of Christ within this text, you must apply the seven years of the temple reconstruction between the years 536–516 B.C. to certain numbers within Daniel 9:24–27. You must remember that the "weeks" mentioned in this text each represent seven years, making it a 490 year total.
>
> Take the 434 years of verse 25 and add the seven years of the temple reconstruction (related to the book of Ezra) and you receive 441 years. Deduct these from the date of the building of the walls of Jerusalem (445 B.C., related to the book of Nehemiah) and you come to 04 B.C., the birth year of Jesus Christ, because the words "Until Messiah the Prince…" (v. 25) refer to the birthday of Christ.
>
> Then take the year of Jerusalem's wall reconstruction (445 B.C.) and add the seven years of the temple reconstruction and you receive 452 years. Deduct them from the 483 years of verses 24, 26, and 27 (in context) and you come to 31 A.D., the crucifixion and resurrection year of the Lord Jesus. So the Lord Jesus Christ lived thirty-five years on earth!

I had been looking only for the birth year of Christ and now the Holy Spirit gave me the death and resurrection year to boot—simply fantastic!

This was not enough—the Holy Spirit then urged me to look for the exact birthday of Jesus Christ. He bade me pay attention to the story of Mary's visit to Elizabeth in the Gospel of Luke 1:39–40: *"Now Mary arose in those days and went into the hill country with haste, to a city of Judah, and entered the house of Zacharias and greeted Elizabeth,"* as well as verse 56: *"…and Mary remained with her about three months, and returned to her house."*

The Holy Spirit told me, *"The reason Mary remained so long with Elizabeth is that in Israel from June until the end of August the climate is extremely hot, not suitable for a pregnant woman to walk so far, about 130 kilometres."* I thought, *"This makes sense!"*

Mary conceived our Lord around May 30, reckoned back 280 days gestation from March 5, which is the correct birthday as proven by information found later in this essay, so she was already pregnant when she travelled from Nazareth. She must have arrived at Elizabeth's home at the latest by the beginning of June. She may have witnessed the birth of John the Baptist in the beginning of September, because Elizabeth was in her sixth month of pregnancy when Mary arrived at her home.

Then the Holy Spirit told me to look closer into Matthew 2:1–12. There we read of a star which led the wise men to Jerusalem to find the newborn king. Generally, it is believed that what they saw was a conjunction of two stars. I have a computer program by name of CyberSky which allows me to see the heavens from any location on earth at any time. So I scrolled the program to the year 04 B.C., centered on Jerusalem. Behold, there were two conjunctions to be seen whose centre fell on March 5, the seventh day of the month of Adar, the last month of the Jewish religious year. These conjunctions tell us directly about the birth of Jesus Christ.

The first conjunction was not visible to the wise men because it happened on a bright day. It was the conjunction of the Sun, Uranus, and Mercury. The second conjunction, however, would have been visible for the wise men up to 9:15 p.m. It consisted of the planets Saturn and Mars.

What do these two conjunctions tell us about the Lord Jesus Christ?

The first conjunction includes the sun (God), the planet Uranus (heaven), and the planet Mercury (the messenger). The message is that God in heaven sends His messenger Jesus Christ from heaven.

The second conjunction includes the planet Saturn (the farmer who scatters seed—compare Matthew 13:3, 24) and the planet Mars (the god of war). Saturn stands higher than Mars. The message is that Jesus Christ, the farmer who scatters seed, is victorious over the god of war: Satan! (See also the book *The Gospel in the Stars* by Duane Spencer, 1972.)

Compare Genesis 15:5, where God shows Abram his descendants. What Abram saw was the star picture of the Virgin whose right hand holds a branch—*tsemech* in Hebrew—and scatters seed from the left hand—*zerah*. This star picture points to the Virgin Mary who scatters seed through her Son, Jesus Christ, the Branch of the Family of David.

It is interesting to learn that these two conjunctions are located within the Constellation of the Fishes. The two conjunctions overlap with each other on the same night, March 5. The fish on the left of March 5 represents Israel, and the fish on its right side represents the Church of Jesus Christ. The Lord Jesus came for both Israel and the Church. The early Christians used the sign of a fish as a symbol of Jesus Christ, as found in the catacombs of Rome. Could there be a connection between the findings above and the use of a fish symbol for Christ? Did the early Christians know of the conjunction and the constellation mentioned above and their relationship to Jesus Christ? According to the information a few paragraphs below, this seems possible.

Did the star of the wise men shine directly unto the house where the Lord Jesus was located? No. At that time they had already a primitive sextant, a tool which the sailors used to find their position on the sea, but it could not pinpoint the exact place. It could not come closer than about fifty kilometres around the location. The star that the wise men saw from Jerusalem to Bethlehem must have been the Holy Shekinah glory of God which could send a light beam directly upon the house in which Jesus dwelled. Except for the wise men, no one else saw this light beam, which is why nobody else could have guided them to the right place. According to Israelite custom as encouraged by the Law of Moses, it is safe to say that Joseph and his family found lodging with a Bethlehemite family on the morning after Christ's birth. They were possibly relatives, since Bethlehem was the hometown of the family of David, and Joseph was a descendant of that family.

In the book *Freemasonry and the Ancient Gods,* as quoted by Gary H. Kah in his book *En Route to Global Occupation,* these words are written: *"In the days of old the Christ came when the point of the vernal (spring) equinox was in the new sign Pisces…"* (pp. 92–93). The only way that the Free Masons of the Middle Ages could have gotten this information is if it was forwarded by some early Christian families.

The official Church did not know about it. Since the sixth-century monk Dionysius Exiguus (500–545 A.D.), the church taught that the Lord Jesus Christ was born on December 25. That is actually nonsense, because the climate in Israel from October to the middle of January has a lot of thunderstorms, hail, and rain, and Jerusalem gets snow about every second year. That is not a good time to travel in Israel, and Joseph and Mary would not have travelled to Bethlehem at that time. Mary was then close to seven months pregnant, so she could not have given birth to the Lord Jesus at Christmas.

Does the idea that the Lord Jesus Christ was born on March 5 conflict with Luke 2:8–12, where it is written that the shepherds were with the sheep in the fields by night? Is the month of March not too early for this? No—March is the first month in Israel when the shepherds are out with the sheep twenty-four hours a day after the end of winter.

Then the Holy Spirit told me to look for the place where the Lord Jesus was laid in a manger. He pointed me to Luke 2:7. It reads: *"And she brought forth her firstborn Son, and wrapped Him in swaddling clothes, and laid Him in a manger, because there was no room for them in the inn."* At the word *"manger"* in verses 7 and 12 is a footnote marked *"feed trough."* This was an important revelation! There were many mangers with the houses in Bethlehem, but there was only one feed trough, which belonged to a certain kind of inn called a "caravansary." Mary had to give birth to our Lord Jesus under the dark sky in the court of the caravansary in the night of March 5, the seventh day of Adar, because there was no room available for them in the inn. Joseph washed the baby Jesus with lots of water, which a Jewish baby required for ceremonial purification, and then he laid Him unto the feed trough next to the animals of travel, the camels, donkeys, and horses. A big help for Joseph was that generally the well in a caravansary is situated close by the feed trough.

Because the angel of the Lord named the feed trough (v. 12), the shepherds had no problem with locating the Baby Jesus, for they knew where that inn was.

As for the crucifixion and resurrection date, the Holy Spirit led me to this information: In the year 31 A.D., the Passover fell on the fourteenth day of Nisan. It was the first full moon after the spring equinox, in agreement with Jewish religious law. The Lord Jesus was crucified on the day before the Sabbath, namely on the fourteenth of Nisan, the first month of the Jewish religious year. He was raised from the dead after the Sabbath on the sixteenth of the month Nisan, in agreement with Christ's statement in Matthew 17:22–23.

In summary: The Lord Jesus Christ was born on the night of March 5 in 04 B.C., the seventh day of the month Adar, the twelfth month of the Jewish religious calendar, in the caravansary of Bethlehem. He was placed into the feed trough next to the animals of burden. He died on the cross on the twenty-sixth of April, 31 A.D., the fourteenth day of the month Nisan, the first month of the Jewish religious year. He was then thirty-five years and fifty-three days old. Both things, the continuous appearance of the number seven in relation to Christ in Daniel 9:24–27, as well as the calendar dates, testify to the fact that all these dates were predestined and controlled by Almighty God.

What I have discovered here was not the product of my wisdom or knowledge, but happened by the assistance of the Holy Spirit, because I could never have found all this information myself! I perceive this as nothing less than a gift of God by His grace.

Based on the information found in this essay, it is easy to determine the actual dates of Christ's Ascension Day and Pentecost. According to the Jewish religious calendar, Christ's ascension happened on the twenty-fifth day of the month of Iyar. Pentecost happened on the sixth day (Sabbath) of the Jewish religious month Sivan. According to our calendar, Christ's ascension happened on Tuesday, June 5, 31 A.D., and the day of Pentecost happened on Friday, June 15 in 31 A.D.

Front View – North

Top View – Front Gate Is North

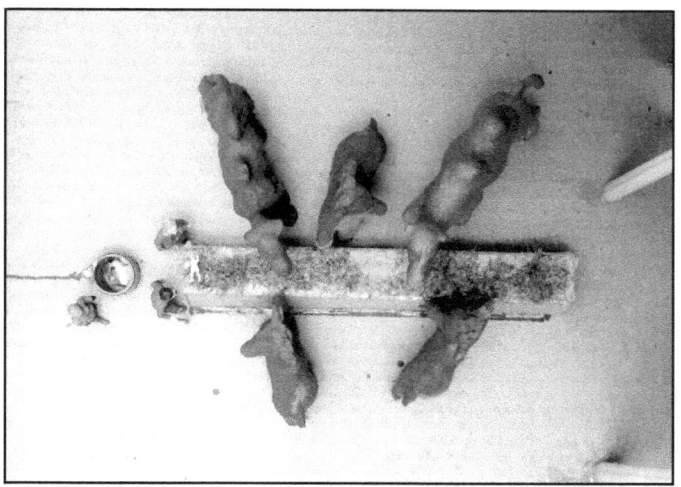
Closeup of Feed Trough

NE Perspective

Inner Court – Looking NW

Inner Court – Looking SW

Figure 17: Possible Model of Caravansary

NOTES

SEVENTY LIES, MISCONCEPTIONS, AND HERESIES CIRCULATED AMONG EVANGELICALS

1. That Sunday is the Christian Sabbath. There is no evidence from the New Testament to claim this doctrine. The Catholic Church is accused of changing Sabbath-keeping from the Sabbath to Sunday, and Evangelicals inherited this doctrine from the Catholic Church.

2. That the Bible holds Sunday rest-keeping to be a Christian duty. This is what the New Testament actually teaches concerning keeping a holy day: *"One person esteems one day above another; another esteems every day alike. Let each be fully convinced in his own mind. He who observes the day, observes it to the Lord; and he who does not observe the day, to the Lord he does not observe it"* (Romans 14:5–6). So the New Testament does not compel us to keep Sundays holy.

3. That everybody in the country should keep Sundays holy. If a Christian chooses to keep a special weekly day holy, it is his personal choice. He cannot expect others to comply with his choice, especially not unbelievers. The Roman Catholic Church, as well as Reformation Protestants, took every person for granted to be a Christian, since they all were baptized as babies, and so they forced all "Christian" nations to accept their Sunday/Sabbath theory, especially because the Sabbath commandment is the fourth of the ten commandments. After former Pharisees told the first Christian Convention of Jerusalem in Acts 15:5 that converts from the Gentiles should be circumcised and keep the Law of Moses, the conference decided that Gentile Christians should only keep the following aspects of the Mosaic Law:

      a. Abstain from things offered to idols
      b. Abstain from eating blood
      c. Abstain from things strangled
      d. Abstain from sexual immorality.

Even the Holy Spirit agreed (*"For it seemed good to the Holy Spirit…,"* Acts 15:28). So it follows also that Gentile Christians need not keep the Sabbath.

4. Adventists claim that Christians should keep the Seventh Day Sabbath. This is also wrong, based on Acts chapter 15 at the Jerusalem Council's decision in verses 28–29, reading: *"For it seemed good to the*

Holy Spirit, and to us, to lay upon you [Gentile Christians] no greater burden than these necessary things: that you abstain from things offered to idols, from [eating] blood, from things strangled, and from sexual immorality. If you keep yourselves from these, you will do well." The reason for this decision was that according to verse 5, *"...some of the sect of the Pharisees who believed rose up, saying, 'It is necessary to circumcise them, and to command them to keep the law of Moses,'"* which includes the Sabbath, of course. Based on that decision, Paul quotes in Romans 13:8–10 five of the Ten Commandments, and writes in verse 8, *"Owe no one anything except to love one another, for he who loves another has fulfilled the law."* He adds in verse 10, *"Love does no harm to a neighbor; therefore love is the fulfillment of the law,"* so Gentile Christians do not need to keep the Seventh Day Sabbath.

5. That sprinkling is the biblical form of baptism. There is no New Testament text that teaches a sprinkling baptism. Basically, baptism is a total body washing as seen in Hebrews 10:22: *"...let us draw near with a true heart in full assurance of faith, having our hearts sprinkled from an evil conscience and our bodies washed with pure water."* The Roman Catholic Church, as well as the Reformation Protestants, used to dunk babies in a baptismal font built of metal or stone. The Greek Orthodox Church still does this today. Nowadays the Reformation Protestants (Lutherans, Dutch Reformed, and like churches) have laid two metal bars across the baptismal font with a shallow bowl on top from which they take a few drops of water to sprinkle on the head of a baby, and they call this a "baptism."

6. That babies ought to be baptized. Churches that baptize babies are called "Paedobaptists," and churches that baptize believers are called "Anabaptists" or "Credobaptists." The Paedobaptists take it for granted that all persons have been baptized as a baby, and therefore an adult "believer's baptism" is a "second baptism" and held to be sinful. Those little children that came to Jesus in Mark 10:14 had not received a Christian baptism, and Jesus told His disciples, *"Let the little children come to Me, and do not forbid them; for of such is the kingdom of God."* So "little" children do not need baptism to be saved. The kingdom of God is theirs.

7. That immersion is the only true form of baptism. Baptists hold this view. However, this is not biblically and historically correct. The biblical baptism is a washing of the entire body, as mentioned in Hebrews 10:22. Where the water is coming from is irrelevant. That is why in early churches found by archaeologists, for example in Masada in Israel, people appear to have been baptized in a bathtub-size baptismal tank where the baptismal candidate was sitting and water was poured over his or her head. This method was used in areas where water is scarce.

8. That you need a clergyman to baptize you. There is no biblical prohibition that would prevent any Christian from baptizing a convert. However, in the New Testament text the baptizers were the apostles and an evangelist because they were the original Gospel tellers.

9. That baptism is a saving sacrament. Baptism becomes a saving sacrament only when it is connected with the faith of the baptismal candidate, as shown in Acts 2:38: *"Repent and let every one of you be baptized in the name of Jesus Christ for the remission of sins...,"* and Titus 3:5: *"...the washing of regeneration..."* Baptism is *"the answer of a good conscience toward God..."* (1 Peter 3:21).

10. That baptism replaces circumcision. This is taught by the Roman Catholic Church and Reformation Protestants. The reasoning is that just as circumcision saved Old Testament children, so baptism saves New Testament children. This false belief must have originated in the church of Corinth, for there they baptized people in place of the dead with the idea that they would be saved, probably for their dead relatives (1 Corinthians 15:22), most likely for their dead children, since at that time many newborn children died very young, and the church believed that baptism by itself saves. In regard to this, Paul says in verse 34, *"Awake to righteousness and do not sin, for some do not have the knowledge of God. I speak this to your shame."*

11. That church membership is unbiblical. Some Church of God congregations and others teach this. Membership in the religious community was inherent in Israel. When a boy or a girl in Israel turned thirteen years old, they were considered to have reached the age of personal responsibility, and they were inducted into synagogue membership. This attitude was transferred by the Jewish Christians to the Church. On the basis of this tradition, Paul can write in 1 Corinthians 12:13, *"For by one Spirit we were all baptized into one body…,"* and the writer of the Letter to the Hebrews can state, *"…let us consider one another in order to stir up love and good works, <u>not forsaking the assembling of ourselves together</u>, as is the manner of some, but exhorting one another, and so much more as you see the Day approaching"* (10:24–25, emphasis added). In 1 Corinthians 5:13, Paul challenges the church to *"put away from yourselves the evil person,"* which only makes sense when they have a membership list like that mentioned in Acts 1:15: *"altogether the number of names was about a hundred and twenty…"* All churches in the New Testament were physically organized congregations and not just a "spiritual" body of Christ.

12. That Communion has nothing to do with the Jewish Passover. This is a false statement, for Jesus instituted the Communion ritual during His last Passover meal celebration. However, most churches do not use the same elements that Jesus used: unleavened bread and alcohol-containing wine. A lot of Evangelicals say that they cannot see Jesus using wine that contains alcohol. This is a misunderstanding of the Passover elements that Jesus used. Traditionally the Jews used alcoholized wine for their Passover meal. However, they did not use this wine in its full alcoholic strength but diluted it with water. A low grade of alcoholic wine is used daily as a thirst-quenching drink in Belgium, France, the Mediterranean world, and the Middle East. Preachers that teach that Jesus used de-alcoholized wine for Communion are either ignorant of the facts or lying.

13. That sourdough and yeast-baked bread can be used for Communion. In Exodus 12, God orders that only unleavened bread should be used for the Passover meal. So it is a sure thing that Jesus followed that rule. Since He used unleavened bread for the rite of Communion, we should do the same and not use leavened or sourdough bread for Communion.

14. That only clergymen should officiate Communion. There is no such rule in the New Testament. Any Christian can officiate the Communion ritual.

15. That only congregational members may partake at communion. Some Evangelical churches give Communion only to their own members. This is unbiblical, for every born-again Christian has the right to partake in Communion.

16. That Jesus did not make alcoholized wine at the wedding of Cana. In the story of the wedding at Cana (John 2), Jesus created a better alcoholized wine than the wedding party had supplied. The Greek word for alcoholized wine, *oinon,* is used in this text.

17. That Christians should not use wine that contains alcohol. In 1 Timothy 5:23, Paul writes to Timothy: *"…use a little wine for your stomach's sake…"* The Bible does not forbid a Christian to drink a little wine, but opposes the misuse of it. Proverbs 23:29 reads, *"Who has woe? Who has sorrow? Who has* *contentions? Who has complaints? Who has wounds without cause? Who has redness of eyes? Those who linger long at the wine…"*

18. That tithing is obligatory for Christians. Paul says in 2 Corinthians 9:13, *"while, through the proof of this ministry [financial giving], they [the receiving Christians] glorify God for the obedience of your confession to the gospel of Christ, and for your liberal sharing…"* and in verses 6–7 he writes, *"…He who sows sparingly will also reap sparingly, and he who sows bountifully will also reap bountifully. So let each one give as he purposes in his heart, not grudgingly or of necessity; for God loves a cheerful giver."* The New Testament encourages Christians to give more than the tithe voluntarily out of love for the Lord Jesus.

19. That *parousia* and *epiphany* are two separate events during the return of Christ. The Greek term *parousia* means "arrival," and the Greek term *epiphany* means "appearance." Pre-Trib proponents argue that the *parousia* will take place when Christ appears the air before the Great Tribulation period, and the *epiphany* will happen when He lands on Mount Olivet after the Great Tribulation. Actually, both events will happen at the same moment when He lands on Mount Olivet.

20. That Christians will never see Antichrist because they will be raptured before he rules. Christ speaks of the setting up of the statue of Antichrist in the temple in Matthew 24:15. And He says in Mark 13:3 that Peter, James, John, and Andrew, disciples representing Christians, would see this happen, so they could not go up in a rapture before this time.

21. That the rapture takes place before the rule of Antichrist and the Great Tribulation. In Luke 17:34–36, Christ speaks of people, some of whom will be *"taken"* and others who will be *"left."* Six European Bible translations, plus the Latin Vulgate, the official Bible of the Roman Catholic Church, clearly state that the "taken ones" go up in the rapture at the end of the Great Tribulation period, and those left behind would go where the vultures would feast on them (Revelation 19:17–18).

22. That the rapture can happen anytime now. Pre–Tribulation Rapture supporters believe that the rapture will happen seven years before Christ's appearance at the end of the Great Tribulation period. Before that happens, the ten-nation Anti-Christian federation must exist. Since it does not exist yet at this time, and the European Union is not the ten-nation federation, obviously the Pre-Tribulation Rapture cannot happen right now. The preachers who say it can are either ignorant of true Bible prophecy or outright lying, hoping that their false claim will make Christians draw closer to God.

23. That there are no specific signs indicating the nearness of the Christ's second coming. There are eight specific signs that will indicate when the return of Christ is near: 1.The existence of the ten nations that will form the Anti-Christian Empire (they have existed since 1918), 2.The existence of the state of Israel (it has existed since 1948), 3.The establishment of the ten-nation confederation, 4. The Great Falling Away, 5. The quick spread of the Evangelical faith around the whole earth, 6. The appearance of Antichrist, 7. The appearance of the False Prophet, 8. The Great Tribulation.

24. That Antichrist will not be a Jew. Israel will accept Antichrist as their Messiah only on the basis that he can show that he is a descendant of the family of David. That is possible because the family of King David can be traced historically until the eighteenth century A.D. During the persecution of the Jews in the 1790s, they went underground, probably immigrating to the USA, where they exist in hiding. Some Jewish clergy may know where they are today.

25. That a German aristocrat will be Antichrist. The Worldwide Church of God teaches this. Since Antichrist is not an "Against Christ," but a false Christ, maintaining he is the true Christ, he will be able to deceive the Jews for a while. He will eventually be seen what he really is—a false Christ. He will copy Christ as much as he can, and will comply with some Old Testament scriptures. He will be born in Bethlehem to a demon-possessed woman. He will probably have a Palestinian mother and Jewish father. He will be assassinated, and even experience a resurrection (Revelation 13:3).

26. That the pope is Antichrist. The pope can never be Antichrist because his personal name does not add up to 666, though his position's title can. We are looking for his personal name, not the name of his title. It is possible that by the design of God a pope's personal name may also add up to 666, but we do not know this.

27. That Antichrist will rule the whole world. This is a misconception because most interpreters of biblical prophecy today do not understand that in the Bible, terms such as "all" do not mean the total, but a part of something (see Daniel 2:39, for example). The size of the earth in prophecy is based on the prophet's knowledge of it, and not ours. Antichrist has enemies like Prince Gog of Magog (Russia) (Ezekiel 38–39), and 200 million soldiers from the East, most likely China (Revelation 9:16).

28. That the Great Tribulation will engulf the whole world. See point 27.

29. That the whole world will accept the number 666. See point 27.

30. That the Church has replaced Israel. Israel's rejection is not total (Romans 11:2); Israel's rejection is not final (Romans 11:15, 29). Israel's final acceptance is found in Romans 11:26. The Church does not replace Israel, but it is a part of Israel (Romans 11:16).

31. That the "elect" in Matthew chapter 24 are only Jews. Pre-Tribbers appear to think that any mention of the "elect" in the New Testament refers to Jews. 1 Peter 1:1–2 appears to refer to the Jews as *"pilgrims of the Dispersion"* and calls them *"elect."* However, when 2 Peter 1:1 speaks of *"those who have obtained like precious faith with us [the Jews]"* it appears to refer to Gentile Christians. The thought is reinforced by 1 Peter 2:6–10, where Peter contrasts the failure of the Jews with *"you who believe."*

32. That the temple has already been constructed in its parts and awaits transport to Israel. This false news was written in a Christian newspaper forty years ago. What is true is that there exists a "Temple Institute" in Israel that has produced the priestly dresses and temple tools, and has plans to rebuild the temple eventually.

33. That the Dome of the Rock must be destroyed to make place for the Jewish temple. Ignorant persons say this. According to archaeologist Asher S. Kaufman, an extant "Foundation Stone" for the Ark of the Covenant has been found and is identified as part of the second temple (Kaufman, 1983). It exists some distance north of the Dome of the Rock, meaning this building does not need to be destroyed to make room for the temple structure. However, God would never be happy with the building of another religion standing on the same ground as the temple, so it will probably be destroyed, perhaps by a missile fired from Iran at Jerusalem and landing accidentally on the Dome of the Rock.

34. That the vultures are increasing fast to be ready for the Battle of Armageddon. This is another lie found in a Christian newspaper forty years ago. In fact, according to Sharon Udasin on July 24, 2017, there are only 180 vultures in Israel, and they are in danger of extinction.

35. That there will be no saved Christians on earth during the Great Tribulation. In Revelation 12:17, 14:1–4, and 15:3, Christians existing during in the Great Tribulation are mentioned.

36. That all people at the White Throne Judgment will be condemned to hell. This is a typical example of Evangelical whimsical interpretation! If all people at the Great White Throne judgment were to go to hell, no mention of the Book of Life would be necessary. Evangelicals teach that all people who have not taken Christ as their Saviour and Lord will automatically go to hell. However, there are Old Testament saints who will live in heaven. There are also millions of people throughout the ages who would have taken Christ for their Saviour and Lord had they been given the opportunity to do so. God knows them, and He will not send them to hell! They are the people who bring their glory and honour to the heavenly Jerusalem (Revelation 21:24), and who need healing (Revelation 22:2) because they are resurrected with fleshly bodies. They do not have celestial bodies like the resurrected Christians have according to 1 Corinthians 15:40 & 52, but will be resurrected with a fleshly body according to the Apostles' Creed.

37. That the Church will not go through the Great Tribulation. As proven above, the Church will go through the Great Tribulation, but it will be protected from the plagues and judgments that Antichrist and the godless people have to go through (see Revelation 7:3–4; 9:4; 18:4). In Zephaniah 2:3 it says, *"… you will be hidden in the day of the Lord's anger."* However, they will experience the wrath of Antichrist, and many members of the Church will become martyrs (Revelation 6:9–11).

38. That Revelation chapters 1–3 represent church history. This is an Evangelical fairy tale, for every church wants to be "Philadelphia," the church that gets the greatest praise from Christ. The seven churches of Revelation 2–3 find representatives in every century.

39. That Revelation 4:1 represents the rapture of the Church. This is another Evangelical fairy tale, for the call to *"Come up here"* of John was not a physical rapture of John to heaven; rather, only his spirit was lifted up to heaven according to verse 2. Not a good example for the Pre-Tribulation Rapture.

40. That in Revelation chapter 1:10, *"the Lord's Day"* refers to a Sunday. This is an error. John was a captive on the island Patmos and thinking about the "Lord's Day" that Christians of his day expected to come in the End Time, and he was wondering if it had arrived. Old Testament prophets wrote about it, as for example in Zechariah 14:1: "Behold, the day of the Lord is coming…" as a judgment day against the nations that would trouble Israel in the End Time. As an answer to John's thinking, Christ gave him the vision of the Lord's Day when He would intervene against Antichrist and the godless world in Revelation 6–19.

41. That the story of Revelation chapters 6–19 runs chronologically. This is a scholarly error, for the second coming of Christ is described five separate times in these chapters, either directly or as a consequence of the text (Revelation 6:16; 11:15; 14:14; 16:16–17, and chapter 19). All three series of seven—the seals, the trumps or trumpets (which are actually battle signals in response to the setup of Antichrist's image in the temple), and the vials of God's wrath—end with the coming of Christ, proving that the book of Revelation does not run chronologically.

42. That Christ and the apostles forbid divorce except for adultery. In 1 Corinthians 7:15, Paul allows divorce of the unbeliever from the believer.

43. That the Bible forbids birth control measures. There is no such commandment in the Bible. However, there is the story of Onan in Genesis 38:8–10. He was supposed to pro-create an heir for his deceased brother, and emitted his semen on the ground to prevent this. Some take this to mean that God is against birth control, but God was not against this form of birth control in general. Rather, God was against Onan's specific act because he did not want to pro-create an heir for his brother, and that was the reason God killed him.

44. That sex is just for procreation. In Ecclesiastes 9:9, the writer says, *"Live joyful with the wife whom you love all the days of your vain life… for that is your portion in life…"* This indicates that sex is not just for procreation. The Song of Solomon is a depiction of erotic love (for example, 7:7–8, 10).

45. That women may not wear fancy clothes. In Ezekiel 16:10–13, God expresses His attitude concerning fancy clothes. He himself would dress Jerusalem with embroidered cloth, fine linen, and silk, and adorn her with ornaments, bracelets, and a golden chain on her neck. In 1 Timothy 2:9, Paul recommends women to exercise moderation with braided hair, gold, pearls, and costly clothing. Peter says similar things to Paul (1 Peter 3:1–5), but adds the example of ancient holy women like Rebekah. Eliezer put a ring on her nose and two bracelets on her arms. The point is that a woman's highest worth should not be found in her clothes, hairstyle, and jewelry, but her character. It is an honour for a girl or a wife when they get jewelry from their family or friends, and it is right to honour them by wearing it. However, they should not show off all their jewelry at once, but exercise moderation like Paul says.

46. That women may not wear jewelry. See point 45.

47. That women may not wear different hairstyles. See point 45.

48. That single women must wear a head covering. In 1 Corinthians 11:3–15, Paul addresses the question of head coverings for women. He uses two Greek words, *gynaikos* and *gyne*. The first word means womanhood in general, and the second generally means a married woman. He emphasises that the married woman should wear a head covering, and that all women should have long hair. However, when praying with her voice, a single woman should cover her head. Otherwise, her hair provides a head covering (verse 15). Looking at the whole teaching, it appears that a head covering is required only of the married woman, and for single women only when praying orally.

49. That any clothing fashions are acceptable for Christian women. The Church Fathers wrote that the Christian woman should dress modestly, not revealing her body's curves so as not to entice men sexually. This makes sense. The modern idea that she should look "sexy" is against the morality of the Bible. It is shameful how a lot of Christian women dress nowadays, even in Church. Christian men should oppose such and tell them to dress modestly.

50. That wives must be subject to their husbands like slaves. In Ephesians 5:22–29, Paul says that the husband is the head of the wife (and family). That does not mean that he should boss her around; rather, he bears the responsibility for wife and family. He is to love his wife like himself, and she is to respect her husband. Peter adds, *"Husbands, likewise, dwell with them [wives] with understanding, giving honor to the wife, as to the weaker vessel, and as being heirs together of the grace of life, that your prayers may not be hindered"* (1 Peter 3:7).

51. That wives must stay at home to do housework and raise children. It is ideal when wives can afford to stay at home to do all that, but the reality of life often means that it would be a big financial help if she could also work outside of the home. My wife has the right idea. She says that a mother should stay at home with the children until they start going to public school; after that, she may go and earn money. This makes sense. In Proverbs 31:10–31, a diligent wife is praised for her enterprise.

52. That Christian couples should have many children. In Psalm 127:3–5, children are called a *"heritage from the Lord… Happy is the man who has his quiver full of them…"* However, I have seen mothers of many children who look sick and deflated. This burden appears to be too much for them. Here too Peter's admonishment to husbands in 1 Peter 3:7 makes sense: *"…dwell with them with understanding, giving honor to the wife…"* However, for one's ethnic heritage to survive, it is necessary that each family has four or five children, for some people will never have a family of their own.

53. That women may not preach and lead a Christian congregation. This is an error that has come about by misunderstanding Paul's intent in 1 Timothy 2:11–12. There Paul says, *"Let a woman learn in silence with all submission. And I do not permit a woman to teach or to have authority over a man, but to be in silence."* In 1 Corinthians 14:34–35, Paul's intent becomes a little clearer: *"Let your women keep silent in the churches, for they are not permitted to speak; but they are to be submissive, as the law also says. And if they want to learn something, let them ask their own husbands at home; for it is shameful for women to speak in church."* On the basis of these statements a lot of Evangelical churches do not have female pastors. However, they create a contradiction between these verses and Acts 2:17–18, where it says that *"your sons and your daughters shall prophesy,"* and that *"on My menservants and on My maidservants I will pour out My Spirit in those days; And they shall prophesy"* (emphasis added). What is prophesying other than preaching? In fact, Paul mentions seven women in ministry in Romans 16:1–15: Phoebe, Priscilla, Mary, Junia, Tryphena and Tryphosa, and Julia, and in Acts 21:9 we read that the evangelist Philip had four virgin daughters who prophesied! So how do we solve this problem? It's easy if you know early church history! Since the first Christian churches consisted of Jewish people, they would have automatically adopted the synagogue order of seating they were used to. The men and boys sat in the middle in the worship hall, and the women and girls sat on the side fringes. So if a woman had a question concerning the preacher's statement, she would holler to her husband in the hall to explain things to her. That is what Paul forbade, since it would disturb the preaching.

54. That Christian women may not speak in a church service. See point 53.

55. That a church should not have a Sunday school. Some extreme Calvinist churches teach that if God wants to get somebody saved, He does not need the Sunday school.

56. That a church should not engage in missions. Similarly, some extreme Calvinist churches teach that if God wants to get somebody saved, He does not need a church engaged in missions.

57. That the foot washing ritual was just for the apostles. Modern preachers say so, but not the early Christians. In 1 Timothy 5:10, Paul mentions *"if she has washed the saints' feet."* This indicates that foot washing was done in the early congregations.

58. That the foot washing ritual is not for the Church in general. The answer in point 57 indicates that foot washing was done in the early church, so it should be practised in churches now. Actually, Christ commands us to do it in John 13:14–15 & 17. I have done this in my church, and I learned a lesson. It is not nice when women pull their skirts up to loosen their hoses and bare their feet for the foot washing ceremony. So I was thinking: the reason why the foot washing was done in the Middle East was not only to clean the feet before entering a house, but also to ease the burning of a guest's feet. They did not wear closed shoes like we have, but open sandals, so their feet were mostly very dusty. Today, we may have the same problem with our shoes entering a house. Therefore we can clean the dust off our shoes before entering a house. This is easily done with a cloth or paper towel, it does not require women to lift their skirts, and the meaning of the act is practically the same as with the original foot washing ceremony, thus fulfilling the meaning of foot washing perfectly. Why did Jesus institute the foot washing as a ritual to the disciples, and what is its meaning? To practice an act of love in humility.

59. That the Bible we use contains no contradictions. This is said because of ignorance, or not wanting to face the truth. In the New King James Version of the Bible, contradictions exist in about 170 places. For example, in Hosea 8:13 & 9:3 it says that Israel shall return to Egypt, and in 11:5 it says that Israel shall *not* return to Egypt. In Galatians 6:2 it says, *"Bear one another's burdens, and so fulfill the law of Christ,"* and in 6:5 Paul says, *"For each one shall bear his own load."* Sometimes the translators create a contradiction unnecessarily, for example as in John 3:13: *"No one has ascended to heaven but He who came down from heaven, that is, the Son of Man."* The truth is that God took Enoch to heaven in Genesis 5:24, and in 2 Kings 2: 1–11, God took Elijah to heaven. The problem is the word *"ascended"* in John 3:13. The Greek word for that word is *anabaino,* which means "to go up by one's own power." No one except Jesus Christ did that, so why could the translators not make that clear by their translation? The great miracle of the Bible is that none of these contradictions have a bearing upon its spiritual teaching, so you can still trust it.

60. That every word in the Bible is inspired by God. All the English Bible translations that I have read claim so, but it is not the truth. The Bible scholar and commentator Adam Clarke says this: *"'All Scripture is given by inspiration of God'* – This sentence is not well translated; the text should render: *"Every writing <u>divinely inspired</u> is profitable for doctrine…"* (Clarke, n.d.). All German, Swedish, and Danish Bible translation that I have read state *"all Scripture**, inspired by God**, is profitable…"* There are some Bible texts that do not need or claim a divine inspiration, like for example 2 Timothy 4:13, where Paul asks Timothy to bring to him the cloak that he left at Troas, along with some books and parchments when he comes. Or 1 Corinthians 7:12, where Paul says, *"But to the rest I, not the Lord, say…"* and in verse 25, *"I have no commandment from the Lord…"*

61. That the Holy Spirit in the Old Testament is of neuter gender. This is not true, because in the Hebrew Old Testament, the Holy Spirit is rendered in the feminine gender. The reason for this is that there exists no neuter gender in the Hebrew language. Because the Holy Spirit is feminine in the Old Testament, some people claim that in fact the Holy Spirit is feminine in gender, but this is a mistake. Christ makes it clear in Matthew 22:30 that in the resurrection people will be like the angels: sexless. Angels are spirits. God is a Spirit (2 Corinthians 3:17), so God is sexless too, and so is the Holy Spirit.

62. That man's likeness of God is mainly intellectual. In Genesis 1:26 it says that God created people in His image. The Hebrew word for *"image"* here is *tselem*, and for *"likeness" demuwth.* Both words focus on outward appearance, not mental attributes. Evangelical preachers teach that when God speaks of his eyes, hands, feet, and other body parts in the Old Testament, it is meant to be abstractly taken. However, in Exodus 24:9–11 the leaders of Israel saw the living God. His feet are especially mentioned. So, according to *tselem* and *demuwth,* we look like God physically. By creation we are God's children already, which means we are a part of the family of God, and thus we are *"gods"* as mentioned in Psalm 82:6: *"I said, 'You are gods, and all of you are children of the Most High…,'"* except that we have fallen in sin.

63. That the creation story in Genesis chapter two is part of the creation story in Genesis one. Many have tried to reconcile Genesis two with Genesis one, but really, no matter how you try, that makes no sense! That is why the liberal and modernist theologians tear all these chapters apart and give them different meanings. I say: why not accept the fact that these two chapters speak of two different creations? The creations of Genesis one began about six billion years ago and continued until the creation of mankind, according to some scientists, while the creation in Genesis two happened about six thousand years ago. In chapter one the creation of mankind is the last creational act of God, while in chapter two the earth already exists, and man is the first creational act God performs. The idea that God created everything six thousand years ago stems from the English bishop James Ussher (1581–1656). He accumulated the list of ancestors of Christ in Matthew and Luke, and arrived at 4,004 years before Christ for the creation of everything. However, the Bible never claims this. The people created in Genesis 1 were the African people created about 300,000 years ago at the Horn of Africa, followed by the East Asian people far earlier than Adam. Adam was created 6,000 years ago, and the Semites and Indo-Europeans first appear after the Flood of Noah about 4,500 years ago.

64. That the Bible says God created everything 6000 years ago. See point 63.

65. That only the original King James Bible is a valid translation. There is a group among Evangelicals, especially among extreme Baptists, that believe the old King James Bible is the only valid Bible translation. This is nonsense. The translators of the old KJV had no access to the recent finds of ancient manuscripts, especially the Qumran manuscripts discovered in 1948. So a number of modern Bible translations, including the revision of the New King James Bible, could be updated and corrected. Also, the language of the old KJV makes it difficult for young people today to properly understand God's Word. That does not mean that all modern Bible translations are good. Most Evangelical pastors and Bible scholars can advise which modern Bible translation to accept, and which to reject.

66. That the second commandment forbids all image-making like statues, etc. The second commandment is directed against idol worship, not any artist's creation that has nothing to do with idol worship.

67. That the second commandment forbids all pictorial presentations of people, including photographs. As in point 66, pictorial presentations of people, animals, or nature that have nothing to do with idol worship are acceptable.

68. That the second commandment forbids all pictorial presentations of animals. See point 66.

69. That the Bible forbids having pictures of God, Jesus, and/or the apostles in church. Pictures representing God should be avoided. Pictures of the man Jesus and other biblical representations like Noah, Abraham, and so on are permissible to have in church.

70. That nobody who is saved can fall away from the faith and be lost again. This is the teaching of Baptists under "Eternal Security." They conveniently say that anyone who falls away has never been a born-again Christian. This begs the question, for Hebrews 6:4–6 clearly teaches that a born-again person can fall away from the faith. Here is what it says: *"For it is impossible for those who were once enlightened, and have tasted the heavenly gift, and have become partakers of the Holy Spirit, and have tasted the good word of God and the powers of the age to come, if they fall away, to renew them again to repentance…"* If they have become partakers of the Holy Spirit, it is clear that the writer of Hebrews means born-again people, and he clearly states that it is possible that such people can fall away and lose their salvation. There is an eternal security available according to John 10:28–29: *"I give them eternal life, and they shall never perish; neither shall anyone snatch them out of My hand. My Father, who has given them to Me, is greater than all; and no one is able to snatch them out of My Father's hand."* The only one who can snatch you out of God's hand is you yourself, because this statement does not overrule our free will. You can slip out of the hands of Christ and the Father if you want, to as indicated in Hebrews 6:4–6. There are no conscripts in heaven, only volunteers!

NOTES

FALLACIES OF THE PRE-TRIBULATION RAPTURE THEORY

THESE ARE THE Pre-Tribulation teachings:

1. Christ will come in a two-stage manner. First, He will appear in the air before the beginning of the Great Tribulation, and second, after the Great Tribulation, He will touch down on the earth on the Mount of Olives.

2. At the last trumpet, Christ will come in the air. The living Christians will be changed and the dead Christians will rise, and both will meet Christ in the air to celebrate the marriage of the Lamb.

3. The Church will not pass through the Great Tribulation, because the Church will not experience God's wrath as the unbelievers do during this time.

4. The Holy Spirit will be removed from the earth before the beginning of the Great Tribulation.

5. In the Great Tribulation, some people will repent and accept Christ as their Saviour and Lord. They will suffer at the hands of Antichrist and become the Great Tribulation martyrs.

6. Christians will not see Antichrist, since they will be removed from the Great Tribulation before it happens.

7. There will be no Christians on earth during the Great Tribulation.

8. Proponents of these views claim that they are proven by one hundred Scripture verses.

Rebuttal:

In the New Testament, the second coming of Christ is first mentioned in the Gospels. In Matthew 24, where Jesus deals with the end time and His return, *no Pre-Tribulation arrival in the air is mentioned,* but only His coming after the Great Tribulation. The same goes for Mark 13 and Luke 17 and 21. One would think that if a Pre-Tribulation Rapture were to occur, it would have been important enough for Christ to mention it!

I can dismiss the Pre-Tribulation doctrine with basically one Scripture passage. I do not need one hundred scripture verses to accomplish this, as Pre-Tribbers claim for their Pre-Tribulation Rapture theory. In fact, Professor Thomas Ice of Calvary University says that there are no Bible verses that clearly state when the rapture is taking place (Ice, 2009). *He is wrong,* for in Mark 13:26–27, the Lord Jesus says, *"Then they will see the Son of Man coming in the clouds with great power and glory. And then He will send His angels, and gather together His elect from the four winds, from the farthest part of earth to the farthest part of heaven."* According to context, this happens at the end of the Great Tribulation. Mark the important words "from the earth… to heaven." Any person who can understand English reasonably well can understand that these words clearly represent the rapture. This is the logical understanding of this text.

The Lord describes the Great Tribulation, which begins from the middle of the treaty of Antichrist with Israel according to Daniel 9:27, meaning the last three and a half years of that treaty. Note his words, completely dismissing the Pre-Tribulation Rapture theory, in Matthew 24:15–16 & 21: *"Therefore when you see the 'abomination of desolation' [statue of Antichrist], spoken of by Daniel the prophet [Daniel 9:27], standing in the holy place… then let those who are in Judea flee to the mountains… for then there will be Great Tribulation, such as has not been since the beginning of the world until this time, no, nor ever shall be"* (emphasis added). He does not say this publicly to the Jews, but privately to His Christian disciples: Peter, James, John, and Andrew (Mark 13:3). The "you" in Christ's speech concerns the disciples and their followers: *us! Not the Jews!*

However, believers in the Pre-Tribulation rapture maintain that Matthew 24:15 pertains to the Jews who will go through the Great Tribulation, but not the Christians. *This is an error.* Christ says to the disciples *"you"* will go through the Great Tribulation—meaning Christians, represented by the disciples of Christ. Pre-Tribbers say that His disciples were Jews. Ethnically this is true, but religiously it is wrong, because the disciples of Christ were Christians who had the highest Christian office in the Body of Christ: they were Christian apostles! And they were told that they would see the image of Antichrist in the temple, and that they should flee to the mountains. This proves that Christians will not be raptured—at least not before this point in time of the Great Tribulation.

Supporting Bible Verses

In 2 Corinthians 5:17 it clearly says, *"…if anyone is in Christ, he is a new creation; old things have passed away; behold, all things have become new."* This says that the disciples as Christians were new creations. Does Christ treat the Jewish Christians differently than Gentile Christians?

Not a chance! In Ephesians 2:18, Paul says, *"For through Him [Christ] we both [Jewish and Gentile Christians] have access by one Spirit…"* And in verse 16, *"…[Christ] may reconcile them both [Jewish and Gentile Christians] to God in one body [the Church] through the cross…"*

The Church began as a Jewish religious institution to which Gentiles were added. Acts 17:1–4 is an example of this trend. It is because of this Jewish element in the church of the Thessalonians that 1 Thessalonians 4:14–17 becomes important to point out that Jewish Christians are raptured at the same time as Gentile Christians.

The sentence *"flee to the mountains"* (Matthew 24:16) indicates that Jewish Christians will not be raptured before the image of Antichrist is set up in the temple, which means that neither will Gentile Christians! Transposed to our time, this means that the Jewish Christians are to flee from Israel to the Kingdom of Jordan, which makes sense since Jordan is not a part of the Anti-Christian Empire.

In Luke 17:31–36, Christ says, *"In that day [referring to His coming]… I tell you, in that night there will be two men in one bed: the one will be taken and the other will be left. Two women will be grinding together: the one will be taken and the other left. Two men will be in the field: the one will be taken and the other left."* In the German Luther translation, this becomes a lot clearer where the word "taken" means in German "accepted," and the word "left" means "forsaken."

What does the word "taken" mean? Compare Genesis 5:24: *"…Enoch walked with God; and he was not, for God took him."* To where did God take him? To heaven through rapture, of course. 2 Kings 2:1 says, *"…it came to pass, when the Lord was about to take up Elijah into heaven…"* See also verses 3, 5, 9, and 10. The people in these verses, and in Luke 17:31–36, were taken in a rapture to meet the Lord in the air, which, according to this text, happens at the end of the Tribulation period. The ones left behind were destined for the wrath of God. The words, *"Wherever the body is, there the eagles [vultures] will be gathered together"* (Luke 17:37), indicate that the bodies of the "left ones" will end up in the destruction of the godless. That should be evident to any reasonable reader! And the rapture in this text is positioned at the end of the Great Tribulation!

Does Revelation 4:1–2 refer to the Rapture?

Pre-Tribbers believe that the "letters to the churches" of Asia Minor in Revelation 1–3 represent the development of the "Church Age," and that John's call to *"Come up here"* (Revelation 4:1) represents the Rapture of the Church. What a fantasy! On the contrary, it was really a personal call to the Apostle John. In verse 2, John explains that he was not physically raptured into heaven, but only spiritually! This is not a good argument for a Pre-Trib Rapture!

In chapters six to nineteen, Revelation presents the events of the seven-year contract of Israel with Antichrist. The story does not unfold chronologically (contrary to what is claimed by a lot of Christian scholars), as proven by the run of the seven seals, seven trumpets, and the seven bowls of wrath, all of which end with the coming of Christ. In the series of seven seals, the coming of Christ is positioned during the sixth seal because of the shortening of the Great Tribulation by 110 days according to Jesus in Matthew 24:22 and Daniel 8:14 where the text says *"two thousand three hundred days."* However, the footnote reference to this verse explains that "days" should literally be translated as "evening-mornings," referring to the sacrifices practiced in the evening and morning of every day, leaving us with 1150 days, a shortening of 110 days for the run of the Great Tribulation.

Pre-Tribbers say that God will rapture the Christians before the Great Tribulation because they will not be exposed to the wrath of God. Well, Christians will go through the Great Tribulation as proven by Revelation 6:9; 12:17; 17:6; 18:6 & 18:24. However, God will protect Christians from the wrath of God during the Great Tribulation, as seen in Revelation 7:3: *"Do not harm the earth, the sea, or the trees till we have sealed the servants of our God on their foreheads."* See also Revelation 9:4: *"They were commanded not to harm the grass of the earth, or any green thing, but <u>only those men that do not have the seal of God on their foreheads</u>"* (emphasis added), and Revelation 18:4: *"And I heard another voice from heaven saying, 'Come out of her, my people, lest you share in her sins, and lest you receive of her plagues.'"*

However, they will be exposed to the wrath of Antichrist, as proven by Revelation 6:9–11.

Pre-Tribbers say that no Christians will go through the Great Tribulation and that the martyrs are unraptured people who converted during the Great Tribulation. But there are no quotations in Revelation 6–19 about conversions of the godless, but to the contrary, quotations that testify about the stubbornness of the godless (Revelation 6:15–17; 9:4, 6, & 20–21; 13:4; 16:2, 10–11, & 21; 17:8; 18:9 & 23).

Matthew 24:15–16 & 21 prove by the word *"you"* that the Christians that exist during the Great Tribulation are converts from the time before the beginning of the Great Tribulation. None are added to their number during the Tribulation!

Pre-Tribbers used to say that the Holy Ghost will be removed before the Great Tribulation, but they changed their belief, now saying that there will be conversions to Christ during the Great Tribulation, and as they know, no conversion can happen without the work of the Holy Spirit.

That the Holy Spirit is still on earth during the Great Tribulation is proven by the presence of Christians during the Great Tribulation, because the Spirit of God lives in Christians (Romans 8:9–10).

Nowhere in the biblical text does it state that Christ will appear in a two-stage way, first meeting the Church in the air and then seven years later landing on earth on the Mount of Olives. Pre-Tribulation Rapture proponents use the story of the ten virgins in Matthew 25 as their argument, which is problematic as it also would prove that the Christians that have no "oil" in their lamps would go into the Great Tribulation. Any teaching of the Bible must be attested by two or more like texts to establish a doctrine according to the Evangelical Rules of Bible Interpretation. This does not happen with the text of Matthew 25. Nowhere in the Gospels does Jesus give a hint about a Pre-Tribulation Rapture.

In 1 Thessalonians 4:14–17, Paul makes it clear that the Rapture and the First Resurrection will take place at the same time, which means that the Rapture takes place at the end of the Great Tribulation, and he says in verse 15 that he received this word from the Lord Jesus Himself. In Revelation 10:7, at the seventh trumpet which ends the Great Tribulation (as confirmed in 11:15), the Rapture is referred to as a *"mystery."* That mystery is explained in 1 Corinthians 15:51–52 as the Rapture, again aligning the Rapture with the First Resurrection. Pre-Tribbers make one hundred Bible verses agree with their doctrine, just like the Jehovah's Witnesses do with their doctrines. In contrast, I agree with what the Bible actually says, as proven with this rebuttal of Pre-Trib teaching. What I present here was the position of the historic Church up to 1830.

Ultimately, this rebuttal proves that the Pre-Tribulation Rapture teaching is a fallacy that cannot be accepted by serious Bible scholars.

MISTRANSLATED BIBLE VERSES

1. Concerning the Rapture

THESE BIBLE VERSES have been translated according to the beliefs of the Bible translators.

> *Then two men will be in the field: one will be taken and the other left. Two women will be grinding at the mill: one will be taken and the other left.* (Matthew 24:40–41)

The word in question is "taken." The Greek term for this is *paralambanetai*. It can be translated to "taken in judgment," but the positive sense of "accepted" is preferable, and the word "left" should be understood as "rejected." Most English Bible translations do translate this word so that it can be taken either way. That is why people believing in a Pre-Tribulation Rapture can get away with their belief. The European Bible translations do not afford the Pre-Tribbers that luxury. They clearly teach an End-of-Tribulation Rapture.

Here is how it reads in the German Luther Bible:

> *Dann werden zwei auf dem Felde sein; der eine wird angenommen, der andere bleibt zurück. Zwei Frauen werden die Mühle drehen; die eine wird angenommen, die andere bleibt zurück.*

> Translation: "Then there will be two on the field; the one will be accepted, the other will stay behind. Two women will turn the mill; one will be accepted, the other will stay behind."

Here it is in the Swedish Bible:

> *Då skola två män vara tilsammans ute på marken; en skall bliva upptagen, och en skall lämnas kvar. Två kvinnor mala på samma kvarn; en skall bliva upptagen, och en skall lämnas kvar.*

Translation: "Then two men shall be together out on the field; one will be taken up, and the other will be left behind. Two women will grind on the same mill; one will be taken up, and the other will be left behind."

Now in the Danish Bible:

Da skal to mænd være sammen på marken; den ene tages med, og den anden lades tilbage. To kvinder skal male på samme kværn; den ene tages med, den anden lades tilbage.

Translation: "Then shall be two men together on the field; the one will be taken along, the other will be left behind. Two women shall grind on the same mill; the one will be taken along, the other will be left behind."

And finally, how it reads in the Low German (Mennonite) translation:

Denn ward twee up'n Koppel wesen un de ene ward good dorvunkamen, un de anner mutt dorbliewen. Twee ward an de Möhl sitten un mahln, un de ene ward good dorvunkamen, un de anner mutt dorbliewen.

Translation: "Then there were two men on the field, and the one was getting away good, and the other had to stay behind. Two women sat at the mill to grind, and the one was getting away good, and the other had to stay behind.

The European Bible consensus is that the rapture will take place at the end of the Great Tribulation.

It is said that John Darby invented the Pre-Trib Rapture by himself. Even a lot of Evangelical scholars endorsed this new teaching so it spread mainly to English-reading peoples, including in North America. The famous British Baptist preacher Charles Spurgeon warned against this new teaching as being false. Christians in Asia and Evangelical churches in Europe reject this new teaching and hold on to the historical teaching of an End- or Post-Tribulation Rapture. The Roman Catholic, Anglican, and Lutheran churches also still teach the Post-Tribulation Rapture, as the Church has taught for 1,800 years.

2. Concerning the Inspiration of the Bible

The prime text for this teaching is found in 2 Timothy 3:16. It reads:

All Scripture is given by inspiration of God, and is profitable for doctrine, for reproof, for correction, for instruction in righteousness…

All English translations of the Bible that I have read state the same.

This is the commentary of Bible scholar Adam Clarke: "'*All Scripture is given by inspiration of God…*' This sentence is not well translated; according to the original Greek reading it should be rendered: '*Every writing divinely inspired is profitable…*'" (Clarke, n.d.). This alternate sentence implies that not every word of the Bible may be inspired by God, as the European translations also indicate.

The German Luther Bible reads:

Jedes Schriftwort, von Gott eingegeben, dient aber auch zur Lehre, Zum Überführen der Schuldigen, zur Besserung und zur Erziehung in der Gerechtigkeit.

Translation: "Every word of the Scriptures *which is* inspired by God serves also for teaching, for conviction of the guilty, for improvement and for training in righteousness."

The Swedish Bible reads:

All skrift som är ingiven av Gud är ock nyttig till undervisning, till bestraffning, till uprättelse. Till fostran in rättfärdighet…

Translation: "All Scripture *which is* inspired of God is also useful for teaching, for punishment, for redress, for bringing up in righteousness…"

The Danish Bible reads:

Etvhert skrift, som er indblæst af Gud, er også gavnligt til at belære, til at irettesætte, til at genoprejse, til at optugte I retfærdighed…

Translation: "Every Scripture *which is* inspired by God is also useful for teaching, to reprove, to raise up for righteousness…"

And the Low German (Mennonite) Bible reads:

Jedes Book, in dat Godd sin Geist lebenni is, hett ock sünst sin Wert. Dat kann uns helpen, dat wi in de rechde Lehr bliewt, dat wi markt, wat gegn Godd sin Willn geit, dat wi wedder up den rechden Weg kamt un in de Gerechdikeit wiederkamt.

Translation: *"Every book, in which* the Spirit of God is living, has also otherwise its value, that can help us, that we remain in the right teaching, that we recognize what is against God's will, that we again come upon the right way and come again in righteousness…"

The emphasis is not that *"All* Scripture is inspired by God," but "all Scripture *which is inspired* by God," just as Adam Clarke explains above. The English Bible translators' bias is clearly revealed by Clarke's explanation and the European translations. There are texts in the Bible that clearly do not need to be inspired—for example 2 Timothy 4:9–22, 1 Corinthians 7:10–16 & 25, and other places in the Bible.

3. Concerning the unnecessary creation of a contradiction

In John 3:13, the translator of the New King James version has created a contradiction. The verse reads: *"No one has ascended to heaven but He who came down from heaven, that is, the Son of Man, who is in heaven."* This creates a contradiction because it is not true that nobody ascended into heaven in the Bible before Jesus, for Enoch (Genesis 5:24) and Elijah both did (2 Kings 2:1–11). The key Greek word translated "ascended" *(anabaino)* means to ascend by one's own power. That is something nobody in the Bible did except the Lord

Jesus. The translator could have made this clear by just saying, "No one ascended by his own power to heaven but He who came down from heaven…" and the problem would be solved.

ONE OF THE GREATEST SPIRITUAL EVENTS OF THE TWENTIETH CENTURY

Pentecost and the Boden/Andersson Spy Affair in Sweden, 1951

I HEARD THIS story from Reverend Oskar Jeske in the Medicine Hat German Full Gospel Church in 1964. It was confirmed to me by a visiting Swedish pastor in 1974, who added more information. The events reported here happened in the year 1951. I will keep this story, which proves that God is still working today, just like in Bible times, as short as possible.

On Sunday, September 23, 1951, Pastor Andrew G. Johnson, pastor of the city of Jönköping's Pentecostal church and one of the early Pentecostal leaders in Sweden, was in his office at 3 PM praying and studying. Suddenly there was a white cloud in his office, and an angel stepped out of it and spoke to Johnson: "I have come to give you a message for your country's government. Please take a paper sheet and write the message down."

So the pastor took those things, and the angel dictated. "In a secret place in the City of Boden's military fort, a spy by the name of Ernst Hilding Andersson is copying secret military documents. He will travel tomorrow to Stockholm, and on Tuesday he will deposit these documents in a bronze hollow post at the gate of the Soviet Union's embassy at eleven o'clock in the morning. Inform Prime Minister Erlander of this."

After informing his wife, Pastor Johnson immediately took the three-hour trip to Stockholm and dropped in on a friend, telling him of the angel's errand. The next morning, they went to the government building where Prime Minister Tage Fritjof Erlander had his office. At the entrance they spoke about their mission to the guard, who forwarded their message to Prime Minister Erlander. He thought Johnson and his friend were religious nuts and made them wait a long time before he would see them. He listened to Johnson's message with little interest until Johnson gave him the name of the secret location, which made Erlander jump up and ask, "Where did you get that name from?" Johnson explained it to him again, and this time Erlander listened with great attention and took notes. He bade Johnson and his friend goodbye and asked them to come back to his office late the next day.

Prime Minister Erlander sent police officers in civil clothing to watch at the Soviet embassy's gate, and they caught Andersson in the act the angel had described. On Tuesday, September 25, Pastor Johnson and his friend returned to Erlander's building and the entrance guard led them very respectfully to the prime minister's office. Erlander also greeted them very respectfully and asked them, "Would you like to see Mr. Andersson?" They agreed, and Erlander led them to a corridor where Andersson sat on a chair between two police guards. Andersson was arrested that day and ended up sentenced to lifetime imprisonment with hard labour, although he was released after ten years in prison.

One day God sent an angel again to Pastor Johnson, informing him that the Russians were planning to assassinate him on a certain day in revenge for what he had told the prime minister. Pastor Johnson informed the police, who hid behind bushes and indoors waiting for the murderer to come. He did indeed come, and the police were able to overpower and arrest him.

Then God sent an angel to him again, informing Johnson that he would pass on to heaven at 3 PM on Tuesday, September 14, 1965. Pastor Johnson called his family together and laid himself down on the couch in his living room on the date indicated, and passed to heaven at the time given by the angel. He was eighty-seven years old when he died.

According to the visiting Swedish pastor I met in 1974, at the same time as the first angel's visit to Pastor Johnson, another Pentecostal pastor living in the city of Västerås, Sweden—I will call him Pastor X, as I forget his name—was also sitting in his office when out of a white cloud three angels, wearing golden crowns, appeared to him with a similar message, adding the name of the spy Fritjof Enbom, and the pressing news that the Soviet Union planned to invade Sweden. Pastor X informed Prime Minister Erlander of this message.

Prime Minister Erlander informed the Swedish government of this threat and the government broadcast the news via radio, newspapers, and posters. The Swedish church authorities asked the people to pray for the salvation of their country. A lot of people did so, unashamedly kneeling down in the streets and marketplaces, begging God to protect them from the Russians.

The Russians sent radio messages that they had other plans now. Sweden was saved from a Soviet invasion by the powerful interference of God's angels.

On Pentecost Sunday May 13, 1951, the Swedish Pentecostals met for the last service of their conference in Stockholm's Philadelphia Pentecostal Church, whose pastor was the famous Pastor Lewi Pethrus, a leader of the Pentecostal movement in Sweden. There was a choir of one thousand pastors ready to sing a song, when a pastor shouted, "I see a big fireball coming upon us!" Seconds later, there was a big bang and fiery tongues fell on the assembly, similar to the Pentecost experience in the Bible. It was the beginning of the first of three Pentecostal revivals happening in Sweden from this day forward.

This event gives credence for the biblical story of the outpouring of the Holy Spirit on Pentecost day in Acts chapter two in the Bible, showing that this is not fiction, but reality—an event which happened on Sunday, June 14, 31 A.D. (The Lord Jesus Christ was born March 5, 04 B.C. and died on Passover, Wednesday April 25, 31 A.D., at the age of thirty-five.)

What does this story teach? It proves that God preferred to use Pentecostal pastors to bring victory for Sweden in its crisis with the Soviet Union. People who reject the Pentecostals should consider this. It also indicates that heaven is real, and is the destination for believers in the Lord Jesus Christ. I have never heard that a similar story ever happened with another religion of the world.

Please note: The three angels with crowns appearing to Pastor X may represent the spiritual powers that are in charge of Sweden's three kingdoms: Norrland, Svealand, and Götaland. On the Swedish coat of arms, these 3 kingdoms are represented with three golden crowns on a blue backdrop. This may be similar to Daniel's vision in Daniel 10:13, 20–21, where national angels are called "princes" of Persia and Greece; additionally, the angel in charge of Israel, Michael, is called *"the great prince who stands watch over your [Daniel's] people"*

(12:1). According to this revelation, it appears that countries have an angel in charge of them politically, and political interference is exactly what the angels in this printed story did.

Dear friend, because this report is one hundred percent correct and true, and has really happened, it shows that the living God indeed saved the Swedish people from domination by the Russian Communists via His angels. Based on this report, you should by now realize that God indeed exists and is a caring person; and I tell you that God is also interested to have you join His family. That is why He sent His only begotten Son, the Lord Jesus Christ, on His mission to make that possible for you. If you are interested in hearing more, please call me, Reverend Werner Trapp at 204-326-9675, and I will show you how to inherit a happy eternity. You can also email me at wtrapp@mts.net.

P.S.: I corrected the timeline of this story with the help of historical and political information via Google, and corrected dates for persons and events. The pictures are public domain. If you wish to access hyperlinked versions of the following references, ask me to email a digital version of this document to you.

NOTES

References

Andrew G. Johnson: https://sv.wikipedia.org/wiki/Andrew_G._Johnson; picture at https://commons.wikimedia.org/wiki/File:Andrew_Johnson-Ek_1910.JPG (Public Domain)

Lewi Petrus (Philadelphia pastor): https://en.wikipedia.org/wiki/Lewi_Pethrus (Public Domain)

Prime Minister Tage Fritjof Erlanger: https://en.wikipedia.org/wiki/Tage_Erlander; picture at https://commons.wikimedia.org/wiki/File:Tage_Erlander_1949.jpg (Public Domain)

Swedish Pentecostal Movement: https://en.wikipedia.org/wiki/Swedish_Pentecostal_Movement

Philadelphia Church: https://en.wikipedia.org/wiki/Filadelfia_Stockholm; picture by Haxpett–Own work, CC BY-SA 3.0, https://commons.wikimedia.org/w/index.php?curid=10255960

Ernst Hilding Andersson: https://sv.wikipedia.org/wiki/Ernst_Hilding_Andersson; picture at https://commons.wikimedia.org/wiki/File:Ernst_Hilding_Andersson_(cropped).jpg (Public Domain)

Picture of Fritiof Enbom at https://en.wikipedia.org/wiki/File:Fritiof_Enbom_1952_(2).jpg (Public Domain)

The Boden Fortress Affair: https://en.wikipedia.org/wiki/Boden_Fortress#Espionage "The other case involved Ernst Hilding Andersson, who was arrested… September 1951. He had carried out seven missions for the Soviets and had provided them primarily with information regarding the Swedish Navy, but also information on the fortifications along the Norrland coast, and an initiated report about Boden Fortress and the air force unit located in Boden and Luleå, Norrbotten Air Base Corps. Andersson was, like Fritjof Enbom, sentenced to hard labour for life."

NOTES

BIBLIOGRAPHY

Abegg, Martin, Peter Flint, and Eugene Ulrich. 1999. *The Dead Sea Scrolls Bible*. San Francisco, CA: HarperOne.

Benton, William. 1967. *Encyclopedia Britannica.* Chicago, IL: Encyclopedia Britannica Incorporated.

Benton, William. 1967. *Encyclopedia Britannica Atlas.* Chicago, IL: Encyclopedia Britannica Incorporated.

Clarke, Adam. N.d. "2 Timothy 3:16," *Adam Clarke's Commentary on the Bible.* Available at https://www.studylight.org/bible/eng/nkj/2-timothy/3-16.html#acc

Dake, Finis Jennings. 1963. *Dake's Annotated Reference Bible.* Savannah, GA: Dake Bible Sales.

Danske Bibelen. 1974. Copenhagen, Denmark: Danske Bibel Selskab.

Darby, John. 1830. *The Morning Watch.* Edinburgh, Scotland: n.p.

Friedrich dem Grossen von Preussen. 1792. *Anekdoten*. Ingolstadt: University Library Eichstätt.

Gordon, John-Stewart. 2013. "Modern Morality and Ancient Ethics," *Internet Encyclopedia of Philosophy*. Available at https://iep.utm.edu/modern-morality-ancient-ethics/.

Grayzel, Solomon. 1968. *A History of the Jews*. Philadelphia, PA: Jewish Publication Society of America.

Henry, Matthew. "Mark 13." *Matthew Henry Commentary on the Whole Bible,* Vol. 5. Available at https://www.biblestudytools.com/commentaries/matthew-henry-complete/mark/13.html

Ice, Thomas D. 2009. "Why I Believe the Bible Teaches Rapture Before Tribulation." *Article Archives* 118. Available at https://digitalcommons.liberty.edu/cgi/viewcontent.cgi?article=1117&context=pretrib_arch

Jessen, Johannes. 1967. *Dat Nie Testament in Unse Moderspraak*. Göttingen, Germany: Vandenhoek & Ruprecht.

Johnson, Peter K. 2012. "Is Revival Emerging in Germany?" *Charisma*. Available at https://charismamag.com/revival/achtung-deutschiand/

Josephus. 1974. *Josephus*. Grand Rapids, MI: Kregel Publications.

Kaufman, Asher S. 1983. "Where the Ancient Temple of Jerusalem Stood," *Biblical Archaeology Review* 9(2):40–59.

Ladd, George. 1990. *The Blessed Hope.* Grand Rapids, MI: Eerdmans.

Lindstrom, Hank. n.d. *BibleLine Ministries.* "Q#1726111." Available at https://biblelineministries.org/q-1726111

Luther Bible 1995. 1995. Stuttgart, Germany: Priviligierte Würtembergische Bibel Anstalt.

Malul, Chen. 2018. "Mark Twain in Palestine." *National Library of Israel.* Available at https://blog.nli.org.il/en/mark-twain-in-palestine/

Nestle, Eberhard. 1945. *Novum Testamentum Graece et Germanice.* Stuttgart, Germany: Priviligierte Würtembergische Bibel Anstalt.

McKeever, James. 1987. *The Rapture Book*. Medford, USA: Omega Publications.

Pallipedia, n.d. "Deontological Ethics." Available at https://pallipedia.org/deontological-ethics/

Rawlings, Maurice. 1991. *Beyond Death's Door.* New York, NY: Bantam Books.

Reese, Alexander. 1957. *The Approaching Advent of Christ*. London: Marshall, Morgan, & Scott.

Scofield, C.I. 1945. *Scofield Reference Bible*. New York, NY: Oxford University Press.

Sinclair, J.M. 1995. *Collins English Dictionary*. Glasgow, Scotland; Harper Collins.

Spencer, Duane Edward. 1972. *The Gospel in the Stars*. Word of Grace Broadcast.

Spurgeon, C.H. 1983. *In Zweite Gedanken (Second Thoughts)*. Kassel, Germany: Onken Publishers.

Svenska Bibeln. 1917. Stockholm, Sweden: Almqvist & Wiksells Boktryckeri AB.

Trapp, Werner. 2010. *The Redemption Story.* Winnipeg, MB: Word Alive Press.

Wiese, Bill. 2006. *23 Minutes in Hell*. Lake Mary, USA: Charisma House.

Wikipedia. n.d. "Bible Translations." Available at https://en.wikipedia.org/wiki/Bible_translations

Wycliffe Bible Translators. n.d. "Impact." Available at https://wycliffe.org.uk/about/impact/

Yehuda, Ben. 1961. *Ben Yehuda's English–Hebrew, Hebrew–English Dictionary*. New York, NY. Pocket Books.

About the Author

REVEREND WERNER TRAPP was born in 1926 in Kassel, Germany. When he was seven, his family emigrated to Sweden to avoid persecution by the Nazi regime. Since his mother was often sick from the burden of immigrant living in Sweden, Werner was often in the foster care of Swedish families. Werner's family was deported back to Germany on November 21, 1938. He followed them when his mother fetched him from Sweden back to Germany at Easter in 1939. In Germany his parents were often hauled to Gestapo headquarters at any time during the night for interrogations. The family stayed out of concentration camp only by the grace of God, but they were constantly under the watchful eyes of the Nazi party.

In 1943, Werner was called in to serve in the German Luftwaffe. He was taken as a prisoner of war after the Battle of Berlin on April 30, 1945. During his time in a Russian POW camp, Werner promised God to go into full time church ministry if God would arrange for him to come home. Within six weeks, he was one of forty out of twenty thousand that the Russians allowed to go home.

Though always a believer in God and the Lord Jesus, Werner was confronted with the reality of the Lord Jesus Christ on November 23, 1946. It was a very strong experience for him, and he immediately sought to find a ministry. He found it as a youth worker for the Evangelical Young Men's Society, receiving his first ministry training at the E.Y.M's Eichenkreuzhaus in Kassel.

In 1952 Werner and his wife Helen emigrated to Canada. The couple has two sons who followed their parents in the Christian faith. Urged on by the Holy Spirit and people, Werner furthered his formal theological education via Moody Bible Institute, Chicago, USA; Northwest Bible College, Edmonton, AB; Steinbach Bible College, Billy Graham School of Evangelism at Wheaton Theological Seminary, and Bible Research International, Cambridge, ON, from where he graduated with a Bachelor of Bible Research diploma.

Werner has always been an avid Bible student. His desire has always been to be right on with God. As such, his goal in his studies is to search for an answer that is Biblically theologically correct. As a Neo-Evangelical, it is his belief that a true understanding of science and scripture must corroborate each other.

www.ingramcontent.com/pod-product-compliance
Lightning Source LLC
LaVergne TN
LVHW081357060426
835510LV00016B/1885